Inside the World of
Board Graphics

SKATE, SURF, SNOW

ROCKPORT

First published in the United States of America by
Rockport Publishers, a member of
Quayside Publishing Group
100 Cummings Center
Suite 406-L
Beverly, Massachusetts 01915-6101
Telephone: (978) 282-9590
Fax: (978) 283-2742
www.rockpub.com

Library of Congress Cataloging-in-Publication Data
Raye, Robynne.
Inside the world of board graphics : skate, surf, snow / Robynne Raye, Michael Strassburger.
    p. cm.
ISBN-13: 978-1-59253-718-1
ISBN-10: 1-59253-718-9
1. Sporting goods--Design and construction. 2. Commercial artists--Interviews. I. Strassburger, Michael. II. Title.
III. Title: Skate, surf, snow.
NC1002.S66R39 2011
741.6--dc22

                                                            2011016457

ISBN: 978-1-59253-718-1 (softcover)
ISBN: 978-1-59253-800-3 (hardcover)

Digital edition published in 2011
eISBN-13: 978-1-61058-1-455

10 9 8 7 6 5 4 3 2 1

Design: Modern Dog Design Co.
Cover Image: Modern Dog Design Co.

Printed in China

Inside the World of
Board Graphics

SKATE, SURF, SNOW

Robynne Raye
Michael Strassburger

WITH

Marty Jourard
Damion Hayes
Shogo Ota
Charlotte West

INTRODUCTIONS BY

Marc Hostetter
Murray Walding
Matt Barr

BEVERLY MASSACHUSETTS

ROCKPORT PUBLISHERS

CONTENTS

Introduction 6-7

LEFT: Board design for Sea
Surfboards. Photo: Paul McNeil.

LEFT: Skateboard deck painted with acrylics and spray paint, inspired by the artwork of Paul McNeil. Client: Christopher Simmons, SFMOMA, 2010. Design/illustration: Robynne Raye.

Introduction

Inside the World of Board Graphics began as a rather unlikely proposition— a counterproposal to another book idea. When our acquisitions editor, Emily Potts, first called she asked us to write a book called *1,000 Board Graphics*. Although the 1,000 series has been quite successful for Rockport, we felt it was the wrong kind of book for us. We wanted to create something with more depth; something that told the backstories of the work. And so the idea for this book was born, allowing us to share the designs of the hundreds of artists whose work you are about to explore.

I already had some involvement with the world of board graphics through Modern Dog, the graphic arts firm I cofounded in 1987. In 1989, the art director of K2 Snowboards gave us a job because he thought we were someone else. That was the beginning of a more than decade-long relation- ship with K2's new snowboard division, during which we helped K2 break away from its parent company's strong image as a ski company. Back then, modern snowboarding was still in its infancy, viewed by many as a fringe or underground sport and banned at most U.S. ski resorts. No one yet had fully realized snowboarding's economic potential, and no one imagined it would eventually become an Olympic sport.

During the making of this book, Art Chantry said something profound to me: "When a sport is brand new, it's easy to be outrageous." Our own

work for K2 was seen as outrageous by some, but more importantly for us, the work was always fun. Modern Dog helped K2 Snowboards develop an ever-evolving identity that separated K2 from the world of skiing—not only visually, but through its branding strategy as well. It was the first client that allowed us to write the copy and art direct the photo shoots. By 1995, our no-holds-barred approach helped K2 Snowboards become one of the largest snowboard companies in the world. This approach also helped my studio gain recognition within the industry as designers who were not afraid to take risks.

Our involvement with K2 came to an abrupt end when it acquired and bought out its competition in early 2000. Within a few months, K2 moved its production overseas and everyone we had previously worked with had moved on. Twenty years later, I am still proud of the work we did for K2 and am thankful we had that opportunity.

As I researched and organized the artist interviews and profiles for this book, something unexpected happened: The project changed how I worked. I became inspired to try new approaches in a way that would not have happened if I had just collected a group of photos for a book. I was humbled by the amazing art sent from all over the world and equally inspired by the people I met. In particular, Paul McNeil's bevy of surfboard art inspired me to paint directly onto a skate deck. By the time this book is published,

I will have taught a skateboard stencil- ing and painting class for high school students through Cornish College of the Arts in Seattle.

Honolulu-based Jeannie Chesser was another artist whose personal story touched me. An avid surfer since 1964, she has endured incredible personal loss, yet through it all has continued to airbrush boards for some of the most respected shapers and pro riders in the world. "Every day I don't surf is like a day off my life" is her mantra.

I was profoundly affected by the discovery of Skateistan (see page 47). Based in Afghanistan, Skateistan is the world's first coeducational skateboarding school, providing art instruction, education, and personal empowerment for young men and women. In the war-ravaged streets of Kabul, this organization has provided a cathartic release for hundreds of Afghani youth who face unimaginable daily struggles.

Then there is Rich Harbour. Rich has the great distinction of a prolific career that began in 1959, and he has produced thousands of boards. He is profiled in the book alongside Australian artist Josh Brown, who was twenty-two years old when we inter- viewed him. Rich's career is more than twice as long as Josh is old. Through my book research on surfing (I bought dozens of books before I began this project), I have never seen this type of juxtaposition: showing the work of a shaper with fifty-one years of

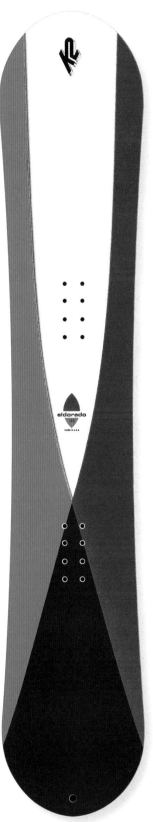

experience along with that of a surfboard artist whose career has just begun. This diverse talent range is what I find so appealing.

Being outside the industry actually gave us an advantage in asking the right questions—which initially I thought were extremely naive— regarding aspects of graphic design that designers, shapers, and artists might take for granted.

Coordinating six writers, dozens of artist profiles and interviews, and hundreds of other contributors from twenty-three countries along with more than 850 images was a logistical challenge. I could not have done it without our fine support staff. I thank them for helping me with the complexity of this project.

The goal of this book is to provide you with a snapshot of what was going on at one point in time in the constantly evolving world of board graphics. The images between these two covers do not exist in the rarefied world of art galleries but are part of the everyday world of snowboarders, surfers, and skateboarders, and for that reason are inseparable from popular culture.

This book is not just for designers, or artists, or even board enthusiasts, but for everyone who finds inspiration in the work of artists doing what they love. My involvement with this project proved to me that some of the most exciting graphics work created today is on surfboards, skateboards, and snowboards. Today's modern art gallery is wherever boards are sold.

Robynne Raye
Seattle, Washington, U.S.A.

Skate

With more than 18 million skateboarders from sixty countries and hundreds of companies producing hard goods for them, the demand for seasonally updated board graphics is staggering. The pioneering nature of skate culture is global in origin, and so are the artists associated with it.

An outsider might imagine that a small talent pool based in Southern California produces all the graphics (consisting of blood and skulls) that comprise the market, but the sophistication of skateboard art transcends all stereotypes and geographic borders. The amount of creativity embedded in this culture is so abundant that it seems poised for the demands of a worldwide movement.

The single most potent outlet for skate art is the deck—a fast-moving, tapping and flipping canvas that becomes an extension of the rider's identity. The body of art itself has many different expressions, reflecting a variety of different types of artists, skateboarders, and for that matter, people. Countless styles and attitudes worthy of an art gallery adorn the laminated and molded wood shapes, expressing good, evil, sarcasm, parody, political views, ethics, ideals, irreverence,

grossness, and even tastefulness. In fact, I've likened average skate shops with their massive displays of decks to art galleries. They're that impressive.

Equally impressive are the artists on the following pages, whose works exemplify the depth and creativity that are so authentic to the culture of skateboarding. There's a distinction in these works of art for all to appreciate but only for skaters to fully understand.

Marc Hostetter
Creative Director, Transworld Media
San Diego, California, U.S.A.

ABOVE: Marc Hostetter, circa 1989. Photo: J. Grant Brittain.

LEFT: Skateboard ramp outside the Muzeum Sztuki, Łód, Poland, 2007. Photo: Hakobo.

𝕸𝖆𝖗𝖙𝖎𝖓 𝕬𝖓𝖉𝖊𝖗 {INTERVIEW}

STOCKHOLM, SWEDEN

TOP: Martin Ander.
Photo: Jens Andersson.

BOTTOM: T-shirt graphic.
Giftorm magazine, 2007.

In 1985, Swedish designer Martin Ander received his first skateboard, a gift from his grandmother. In the early 1990s, soon after breaking into the Swedish graffiti scene, Ander began working with a variety of Scandinavian skateboard companies as well as streetwear brands such as WeSC in Sweden. Ander is also art director of *UP*, a Swedish graffiti magazine, and he runs his own skateboard company, Polygon.

You have a background as a graffiti artist, and you also work as art director for UP. Is there a strong graffiti scene in Sweden, and what is its relationship to design?

Graffiti began appearing here around 1984, when movies like *Style Wars* and *Beat Street* spread the culture around the world. I started getting interested in graffiti in 1987 after seeing the book *Subway Art* at the Stockholm Art Fair, but I didn't start writing until 1991, when I met some other writers who showed me the tricks of the trade. Back then, Stockholm had one of the best scenes

in Europe—the transit and city streets were bombed and you saw train pieces almost every day. In 1992, some older writer friends of mine started UP (then called *Underground Productions*), which was amazing—there were only a handful of graffiti magazines back then. Over the years, the *UP* crew has transitioned to a book publisher and distribution company for subculture and art media (Dokument Press). They do great books and DVDs and stuff. A few years ago, they asked me to take over the production side of UP, and I did.

It seems that the connection between graffiti and skateboarding is important for you. What is the relationship between your background as a graffiti artist and the skateboard graphics you do now?

I grew up with art and graphic design—my dad is an illustrator and art director, and he collects books on illustrators and graphic designers. When I was a kid, we often went to art fairs, museums, and galleries. I liked looking at the pictures and was fascinated with the motifs and techniques, but I didn't get the deeper meaning—to me it was just pictures.

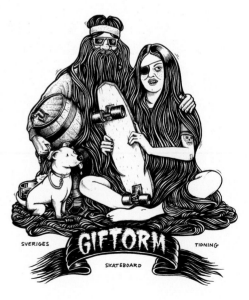

LEFT: "Keep Your Scene Clean,"
skateboard graphic. Sweet
Skateboards, 2009.

MIDDLE: New Age model.
Polygon Skateboards, 2010.

RIGHT: Skateboard graphic. Seven
Inch Skateboards (Finland), 2010.

TOP: Sweet Fighter series. Left to right: Erik Pettersson vs. Anton Myhrvold model; Koffe Hallgren vs. Daniel Spängs model; Björn Holmenäs vs. Martin Pennlowe model; Jonas Skröder vs. Josef Skott Jatta model. Sweet Skateboards, 2009.

LEFT: Skateboard Wheel Graphics (Polygon EGGS). Polygon Skateboards, 2010.

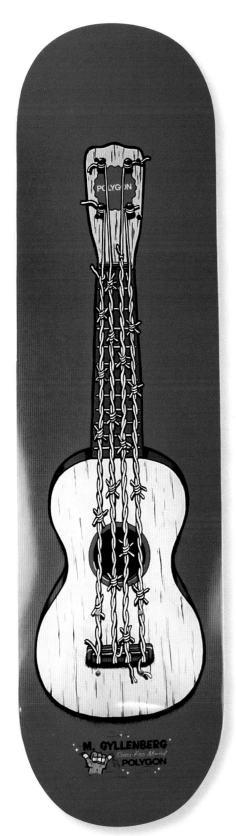

Then I saw the book *Subway Art* and was totally blown away. It spoke directly to me—not just the art, but also that the art was painted by kids, and wherever they wanted. Also, the combination of lettering, cartoon characters, pop-culture motifs, and more serious matters was everything I liked, all melded together.

The same year, I discovered skateboard art, and it was the same feeling. It felt like just by liking these images you were part of something, and they were easy to understand—there were no hidden messages. They spoke to me like the best comic book, but condensed into just one frame and then printed on the coolest thing I could imagine. In the early nineties, when skateboarding went underground, graffiti influences began appearing in skateboard graphics and ads. This was around the same time I made my graffiti debut. For me, skateboarding and graffiti had some kind of connection for some years.

Even though I try not to use graffiti elements in my skate graphics, and I don't see a clear connection between graffiti and skateboarding nowadays, I must say that if I hadn't experienced those years in the early to mid-nineties, the designs I do would look very different.

How did you start doing skateboard graphics? When was your first commission?

I got my first board from my grandma in 1985, after nagging my parents for as long as I can remember. It was a small plastic board that I rode for two years. It had "Skateboard" written on the top in an '80s semigraffiti style. I thought it was the coolest thing ever, until I set foot in a real skate shop, Rip City in Santa Monica, on a holiday trip to Los Angeles in 1987. I could have stayed there all day just looking at the graphics. As soon as I came back to the hotel, I started sketching skate graphics. I also bought my first "real" skateboard there, a Santa Cruz Rob Roskopp deck. I didn't get to make a proper skate graphic until 2007, when my buddies started Bellows Skateboards and asked me to do some graphics for them.

What kinds of techniques drive your design? And what is the relationship between hand drawing and technology in your work?

I use both hand-drawn ink lines and computer graphics in my work. It depends on what I want to do, but I always begin by sketching with pen and paper, then I use whatever is necessary to turn the sketch into a graphic. The process usually includes ink, paper, camera, printer, scanner, Photoshop, and Illustrator.

Do you have any particular themes that you like to explore in your work?

I would like to think that I don't, but my work usually contains some elements of dark humor and irony. I also like to include some personal references in everything I do.

What attracts you to skateboard graphics as opposed to some other form of graphic design?

I think it is because skateboard graphics are more than just images made to sell skateboards. A skateboard graphic printed on something other than a skateboard is just an image, but printed on a skateboard, it becomes part of a more than thirty-year-old design tradition. You put more into it than just the lines and color. It's the profile of the company, the attitude of the rider, and the whole feeling of being a part of a subculture—kind of like when you look at a great album cover or a gig poster and you connect the image with the music and attitude of the artist it promotes.

Another attraction is that most of the skate companies are skater owned and for that reason, less corporate. It doesn't feel like doing commercial work, it feels like being a part of the culture.

What are you currently working on? What companies do you work with?

I'm currently working on a new series of decks for my own company, Polygon. I just finished some T-shirt designs for Spitfire Wheels and a T-shirt graphic for Servant Footwear.

TOP: Magnus Gyllengerg Pro Model. Polygon Skateboards, 2010.

RIGHT: "Transylvanian Transition," T-shirt graphic. *Transition* magazine (Sweden), 2010.

FAR RIGHT: T-shirt graphic. Seven Inch Skateboards (Finland), 2010.

OPPOSITE PAGE: Inside the Morning Breath studio: Jason Noto (left) and Doug Cunningham (right), 2010.

LEFT: Morning Breath "Early Bird Icon," 2002.

RIGHT: Deck for Atlas, "Artist series board design," 2010.

Morning Breath is the name of a two-man design studio based in Brooklyn, New York. Jason Noto and Doug Cunningham first met in San Francisco while working for Think Skateboards, deciding in 2002 to strike out on their own to "do the work we love for people we like." Their collaborations include working with companies such as Atlas, Zoo York, Adrenalin Skateboards, and Circuit Wheels.

Take us through a typical day at Morning Breath. What does your space look like, when does your workday start, and what kind of projects do you work on?

Our days at Morning Breath are anything but typical. We usually arrive between ten and eleven o'clock in the morning. A lot of our projects are bicoastal, so it makes sense to start late and end a bit late. Most of our days begin with a quick powwow to discuss what needs to happen that day—which project is on fire.. Some days, our projects are straightforward design; other days, they are looser, a blend of illustration and our brand of design. When we're waiting on feedback from a client, we'll use that time to take care of the business side of things—invoicing, catching up on emails, sending out orders from our store, and so on. We also do a lot of painting and personal projects. Finding time for those projects can be challenging, but we've become pretty good at juggling.

Our studio is on the tenth floor of a building on the Brooklyn waterfront. We have a really cool view of Manhattan outside our window. The inside of the studio is divided into a painting/make-a-mess space near the windows in the rear and a more organized computer/workstations space in the front. In the center, we have a pool table for those moments of procrastination.

I read that you tag team when you create work. Noto does the design and Cunningham the illustration.

Can you describe your process for creating a board design?

A lot of our style and method for creating board graphics is similar to how we did it at Think Skateboards in the mid-nineties. If we have a solid concept or are creating a very loose abstract design, we usually start with an illustration of some sort and typographic elements. For a lot of our work, we want to achieve a slightly vintage feel, and to do this we use an archive of old typefaces along with specific techniques. Once the design and illustration are put in place we both give it a critique, and share suggestions and opinions on making it better.

Have you noticed any difference in the design culture between the West Coast and East Coast?

We met while working at Think in 1996 in San Francisco. At the time, most skateboard companies were on the West Coast. The East Coast skateboard scene had been growing, but wasn't yet as big as the California scene. Over the next decade, the scenes began to merge, with many people in that industry going bicoastal, including the pro skaters. This brought the urban street culture of New York City to the skate scene of California, which was still a bit more "punk rock" and vice versa. This merging of influences is now apparent in the graphics on boards—they are no longer regional.

It's rare to find such a strong partnership as professionals and friends. Why do you think you work so well together?

We have a tremendous amount of respect for each other, and when we walk into the studio, we leave our egos at the door. We have our moments, as I assume most business partners do, but any differences are settled quickly, and neither of us will hold a grudge. We both take pride in our work; but work is not everything. Both of us have families, and over the years, I suppose we have become family as well.

TOP ROW: Line of decks for Zoo York, Hell's Kitchen Bunch, 2010.

LEFT: Designs for Gold Wheels "Gold Champions," 2010.

Some of your work looks like a visual dumpster. What are your influences and where do you get your imagery?

A lot of our work is influenced by advertising art from the fifties up to the seventies. We sometimes work with found type, and/or we create new type to deliberately look and feel old. We also create cartoon characters in a style that feels very 1950s. Our twist on it is to take the very happy and innocent feel of that era and turn it on its head. We often have the characters look a bit derelict—always smoking and drinking booze, broken teeth, scratched up. Throw in some vintage Times Square–era porn, and *voilà!*

What is the most satisfying aspect of your job?

The recognition we've been getting over the past few years. When we were coming up in this industry we read all the latest design books, illustration annuals, and communication arts magazines. We admired many of the graphic artists of that time, and now it feels good to be featured in those media ourselves. We never imagined that people halfway around the world would be paying attention to our work.

Looking back, what are some of your favorite decks and why?

Our favorite deck designs are probably the Hell's Kitchen Bunch series we did for Zoo York. That particular series was an opportunity for us to do the style and content we have the most fun with. When we worked at Think, we were relative newcomers to graphic skateboard design and we were still learning the digital design process. So many times in life you have those "If-I-only-knew-then-what-I-know-now" moments. The Zoo York series let us do what we would have done a long time ago if we had only known how.

Why did you name yourself Morning Breath?

One night we were hanging out having a few beers, talking about our new business, and realized we needed a name. We were listening to music and put on a seven-inch record from a friend's band named Sweet Diesel. The name of the song was "Morning Breath." We didn't have to think about it any further. "Morning Breath, Incorporated. Yeah, fuck it!"

OPPOSITE PAGE: A variety of decks
for Think Skateboards, 1995–1998.

TOP: Girl Skateboards/Mass Appeal
"Make the Logo Wooden" Exhibition,
2007.

RIGHT: Roller Blader Hater Line art
illustration for board graphic, 1997.

OPPOSITE PAGE: Self-portrait. Photo: Hakobo, 2010.

TOP ROW: "Radio." Client: Pogo Skateboards, 2010.

TOP ROW: "Revolution." Client: Pogo Skateboards, 2010.

TOP ROW: "High Voltage." Client: Pogo Skateboards, 2010.

TOP ROW: "Bomb." Client: Pogo Skateboards, 2010.

BELOW: "High Voltage" (close-up). Client: Pogo Skateboards, 2010.

BOTTOM: Trucker caps. Client: Pogo Skateboards, 2005.

Hakobo {INTERVIEW}

ŁÓD, POLAND

Hakobo is a prolific and highly successful graphic designer from Poland. His images are present in many forms, including bold skateboard graphics. In 2010, Hakobo published his first monograph, *HGW: Hakobo Graphic World*. His often-minimalist graphics are inspired by constructivism, avant-gardism, pop art, psychedelic art, hip-hop, and video games. For the past five years, Hakobo has worked with Polish skate company Pogo.

What does Hakobo mean?

It's the phonetic version of the name Jacob in Spanish (Jakobo).

How does your skateboard design work differ from your other graphic design work?

The most important thing in designing skateboards is the characteristic shape and proportions. I try to use minimal graphics to create a maximum impression. For me, format and composition are the most important things in designing.

Do you have any favorite boards/projects?

I like pure maple wood, covered with straight lines and shapes, as in Pogo's latest collection.

What was the first board you designed?

It was in 2004, the first collection for Pogo. Piotr Dabov [Pogo's owner] and I decided to use three colors in the collection, so we added orange to basic black and white. We were strongly inspired by the classic movie *A Clockwork Orange*.

How did you begin working with Pogo?

It was a story of old friends. In the early 1990s, Piotr Dabov and I were among the first true hardcore skaters in our hometown. Then I became more interested in graphic design than skating. Piotr was always passionate about skateboarding, and in 2003, he started a company called Pogo. After being out of touch for ten years, we met in mid-2004 and spontaneously decided to work together. At the beginning, I treated it as a typical commission, but soon realized that it was going to be a big deal.

LEFT: "Niemaludka."
Client: Pogo Skateboards 2005.

MIDDLE: "Niemaludka."
Client: Pogo Skateboards 2005.

RIGHT: "Teamdeck."
Client: Pogo Skateboards 2008.

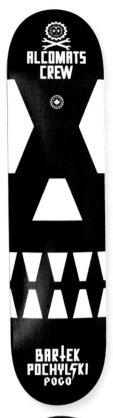

TOP ROW, LEFT TO RIGHT:
"Electro." Client: Pogo Skateboards, 2006. Pochylski Pro Model. Client: Pogo Skateboards, 2006. "Fabrik1." Client: Pogo Skateboards, 2007. "Stars." Client: Pogo Skateboards, 2007. "8ball." Client: Hakobo Ltd., 2007. "Scratch." Client: Pogo Skateboards, 2007.

BOTTOM ROW, LEFT TO RIIGHT:
"Skull." Client: Pogo Skateboards, 2006. "Lion." Client: Hakobo Ltd., 2007. "Grrr." Client: Pogo Skateboards, 2005. Pochylski Pro Model. Client: Pogo Skateboards, 2005. Pochylski Pro Model. Client: Pogo Skateboards, 2005. Baranowski Pro Model, 2008.

FAR LEFT: "Orange."
Client: Pogo Skateboards, 2005.

LEFT: "Orange." Client: Pogo
Skateboards, 2005.

OPPOSITE PAGE: "Skeletors."
Client: Pogo Skateboards, 2007.

Have you done any artistic boards?

Piotr had a very close relationship with Industrial Skateboards, a board manufacturer in the Czech Republic, and I ordered a few blank boards from them. I sprayed them using a stencil. Of course, those boards were rideable, and a few were even used in a skate video for Pogo.

What is the Polish skate scene like?

It all started after the fall of Communism, so Polish skateboarding missed the bowls and backyard ramp era. In Poland, skating emerged from the DIY rebel punk style and was closely related to Polish hip-hop in the late 1990s. Then, at the beginning of the twenty-first century, after strong influence from companies such as ZERO, the punk style came back. What differentiates the Polish scene from that of other European countries is a strong need to have original local brands and media.

The funny thing about the scene is there are big differences between regions. For example, in my town of Łód, the second biggest city in Poland, you can describe the skating style as speed, air, guitars, and tattoos, with an industrial, heavy factory, gray town twist. This is in contrast to the capital of Warsaw, which has a full-color, technical hip-hop style.

𝔐𝔞𝔵 𝔙𝔬𝔤𝔢𝔩 {INTERVIEW}

NEW YORK, NEW YORK, U.S.A.

Max Vogel's creative process involves a key component: music. You can see it in his hand-drawn type and the flowing rhythm of his designs. The images created by Vogel through Razauno, his New York City–based studio, spring from a love of music, skateboarding, and psychedelia, and his early years growing up in Venezuela. Vogel's visual aesthetic combines loose, seemingly casual ideas with precise technical execution. This approach has proven to be appealing to a variety of clients, including 5boro NYC, Zoo York, Upper Playground, MTV Latin America, AKA books, *Complex* magazine, and Sixpack France.

Do you skate? If so, what was skating in Venezuela like compared to the United States?

I learned to skate in Venezuela when I was thirteen, and things were completely different back then. There were no shops and nobody was supporting the scene, so we used to order decks from anyone who was going to visit the United States. Some of my friends would buy used Santa Cruz decks and cut them to get a better shape. The boards were super-heavy, but it was fun because nobody cared about where you skated since cops didn't really know about it yet. Now there are a few skate parks, shops, skate brands, and even an online magazine [www.7capas.com], and the kids are really good.

When you were young, did you think about graphics?

One of the main reasons I got involved in design was because I was fascinated with the graphics on boards and on records. When I was growing up, the design culture in Venezuela was really big. The logos of companies, banks, and public services were designed by awesome people such as Nedo M.F., Gerd Leufert, Alvaro Sotillo, John Moore, and many others who were having fun doing identity in a kind of new country, when there was a lot of big money from international oil companies.

How did you get involved with designing board graphics?

As soon as I moved to New York City, I met Mark Nardelli, one of the owners of 5boro. We became

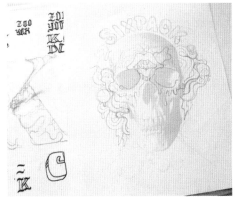

TOP: Sixpack T-shirt. Client: Sixpack France, 2009.

BOTTOM: Sketch for Sixpack T-shirt. Client: Sixpack France, 2009.

FAR: Skateboard deck, "Apple a Day." Client: 5boro.

FAR RIGHT: Skateboard deck, "Stacked Boroughs." Client: 5boro.

friends and I helped him with a few graphics—rather than a regular freelance job, it was more of a group of friends making graphics without rules for a brand we really liked. From there I met with other companies (Zoo York, Maloof Money Cup, CCS, etc) and started working with them.

Does music play a role in your creative process? If so, what do you listen to when you work?
Music is the most important thing for me. Every song is a memory of a time and experience that I like to remember. Through music, I've learned about the link between good artwork and good music. When I was growing up, my dad listened to heavy seventies salsa music and those album covers were sick, especially the type. The music on older skate videos is

really good—Jimmy Cliff, Roy Ayers, Coltrane, Soul of Mischief, Wu Tang Clan, and so on. Lately, I've been listening to salsa: Ray Barreto, Hector Lavoe, Mongo Santamaria, Joe Batan—soulful stuff, guys playing an awesome mix of jazz and Latin in New York City in the seventies. I think it's really badass, especially the lyrics . . . Back in the day, New York was a really tough city, especially for Latinos.

Do you have any favorite album covers?

Oh, man! Too many; here are a few. Izzy Sanabria was the mastermind behind the covers of some of my favorite Fania albums: Willie Colón's *The Big Break*, *Siembra*, and *The Good, the Bad, the Ugly*; Ray Barreto's *Power*; and of course, Pink Floyd's *Dark Side of the Moon*.

Who or what are your design and art inspirations?

Music is one of my biggest inspirations and always a source of great ideas for me, from the lyrics of a song to the cover of an album. I'm obsessed with designers such as Milton Glaser, Saul Bass, Tony DiSpigna, and Bob Gil.

How much of your process is by hand?

I always begin an illustration with a rough hand sketch. For me, it's the best way to lay out type and get the right composition. From there, I will redraw

it more cleanly before it goes to the computer. If I'm not happy with the result, I'll print what I have and draw on top of it. For type, the best thing is to draw by hand. There is something great about a typeface that is imperfect or uneven; it feels organic and always looks better on a layout, at least with my graphic style.

What do you take into consideration when designing a board graphic?

A board graphic always needs to be bold, and because the board is a long surface, you must shape your art to fit it in a way that feels appropriate and natural.

How did you become involved with laser etching on skateboards?

Two years ago, Luca Lonescu invited me to contribute to REFILL 7, a show of all laser-etched skateboards. He assembled a great group of artists and made these boards happen with a laser machine. I had been messing around with one and knew how much detail you could get with them, so I was really pleased to be part of the show.

Is the medium the message? What would that message be?

The message would be to go out and skate as much as you can.

OPPOSITE PAGE: Laser-etched custom deck for REFILL 7 group show, Sydney, Australia. Curator: Luca Ionescu, 2009.

TOP: Laser-etched custom deck for REFILL 7 group show, Sydney, Australia (detail). Curator: Luca Ionescu, 2009.

BOTTOM: Sketches for "Accept Loss Forever" T-shirt design. Client: Sixpack France.

Emil Kozak {INTERVIEW}

BARCELONA, SPAIN

After five years at an ad agency in Copenhagen, Emil Kozak took the freelance plunge, and at the same time, he became a love immigrant to Barcelona to be with his Spanish girlfriend. This lifelong skateboarder-turned-designer has produced more than a few board designs for clients such as Vans, Element, Graniph, Eastpak, Burton, Channel Islands, Nike, LAB Skateboards, and Uniqlo. Steeped in the Scandinavian design tradition, his work features clean lines and typographic treatments, and he enjoys playing with words, codes, and cryptic messages.

You are also a skateboarder. How did you translate your hobby into your profession?

I wanted to make graphics that had some relation to me personally. After too many years in the rat race, I needed some projects that fulfilled that desire. I contacted my friends at LAB—I skated with them as a kid—and we started to make boards.

What was your first commission?

In fourth grade, one of the teachers at my school commissioned me to make drawings that later would be translated into big painted pieces on the walls of the schoolyard. They paid me with a gift certificate to the local bookstore. I ended up buying markers and comics.

The Danish design tradition is known for its minimalism, which is apparent in some of your graphics. Do you acknowledge this influence in your work or is it more implicit?

I love simplicity. I like to speak clearly and precisely about a certain theme. I feel simplicity does that.

What is your process for creating a board design?

Concept, sketching, computer—in that order.

Are there any particular issues or themes you like to play with in your designs?

I've been fortunate to have no restrictions in my skateboard work. I work with themes I relate to personally, such as childhood, growing up, good things, and war and violence, or whatever strange dream I had the night before.

What's it like working as a designer in the skate industry? How does it compare to working in the surf industry?

Seems kind of similar from my experiences. The skate world is more progressive and less conservative, but things are about to change now, it seems.

What have been some of your favorite board designs and why?

The Kindergarten Legends came from ideas I had when I was in kindergarten. I remember we used to tell stories about other kids who had apple trees growing in their tummies, because they had swallowed the seeds from an apple. We actually believed it. I love the surreal imagination that kids have.

I noticed on your website that you have been experimenting with skateboard prototypes (industrial design) as well as one-off hand-painted boards. Can you tell us more about these? Are these for clients or are they personal projects?

It is a project I am working on with Element. Right now we are collecting pro-rider boards from the Element team members. This fall, I am going to reshape and paint them. The ones I've been experimenting with are great boards.

In another interview I read, you mention that what attracted you to the skate industry was its creativity. Can you elaborate on that?

I think skateboarding is a very creative game. It's about making something out of nothing. A skateboarder sees a playground, when other people see an empty parking lot. It is like this imaginary world that you can go to when the other one sucks.

In discussions I've had with other designers, one of the biggest drawbacks for those working in board graphics is the difficulty of making a living at it. Designers get paid pennies in relation to what boards are sold for, especially within snowboarding. Is this also the case within the skate industry?

Yes, it is difficult to make a living out of only making boards, but the wicked thing is, you get work from other companies, probably because they need a bit of "edge" to their profile. There are some strange dynamics going on there.

TOP: Designs for a series of boards, bags, and wheels for Flow, 2008.

OPPOSITE PAGE: Emil Kozak in his studio, located in the neighborhood of Sant Antoni of Barcelona. Photo shot in 2009 by Selftimer.

TOP: Close-up of LAB, 25th Century series, 2006.

LEFT: Skate deck design for LAB, part of the 25th Century series, 2006.

OPPOSITE PAGE TOP ROW, LEFT TO RIGHT: Deck designs for LAB, A Kindergarten Legend (series), 2006–2007. "Remember the days, when the rain was the clouds peeing? And if you ate the seeds of an apple, an apple tree would grow in your stomach? Or the changes of the moon were caused by a man who was eating from it? God shooting lightning bolts at the kids from the sky? The monsters under your bed? Playing doctor? I do."—Emil Kozak.

OPPOSITE PAGE BOTTOM ROW, LEFT TO RIGHT: Skate deck design for LAB, "Cowboys & Indians," 2009. Skate deck design for Element, 2008. Skate deck design for Flow, 2007. Skate deck design for Instant Winner, 2008 Skate deck design for LAB, from the Anatomi series.

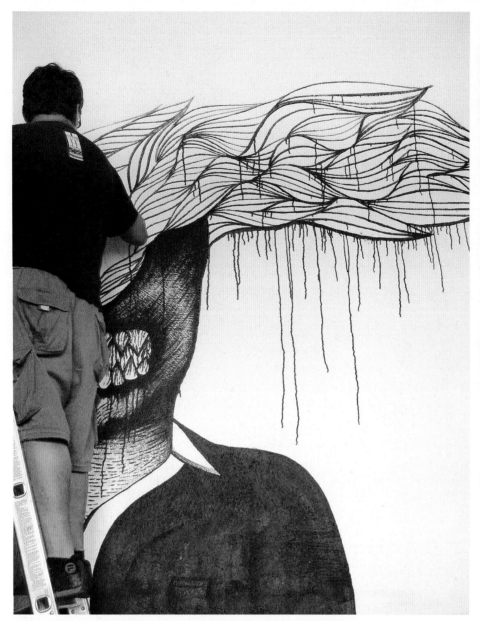

Edgar A. Reyes Ramirez {INTERVIEW}

MEXICO CITY, MEXICO

Inspired by Milton Glaser's "Good Design Is Good Citizenship" philosophy, designer Edgar Reyes created and edited *UNDO*, the bimonthly Mexican magazine of graphic design and art, with a focus on social and cultural issues. These same themes are carried over into Reyes's skateboard designs, where he works in traditional "street style" using acrylics and spray paint. "I am a graphic designer who likes to play with the meaning of words and images," explains Reyes.

What is your background, and what prompted you to get into designing skateboards?
Soon after graduating from college in late 1999, I began to work at one of the most prestigious

design studios in Mexico, La fe ciega [The Blind Faith], a studio specializing in editorial design and, specifically, magazine design. We worked for most of the important Mexican publishing houses, doing redesigns and image consulting. By early 2005, I had become tired and bored after five years of commercial work, so I decided to make a change and do something different. I moved back to Puebla and began freelancing and teaching part time with the idea of having clients I could really identify with, and to do projects that I really enjoyed, such as designing concert posters. At this time, I began designing some custom skate decks.

UNDO is a nickname you go by. Please explain where this came from.

Around 2005, I began to shape the *UNDO* project, a personal project that allows me to explore integrated processes. Most of the *UNDO* series concepts begin in a notebook, with sentences or stories, which I later illustrate—usually with black ink or rollerball pens. I never consider it important to create a continuous graphic style, because it's more interesting for me to enhance the specific content. Once I decide on a style, I design a complementary typeface, as almost all my images contain phrases. Instead of having a source of inspiration, *UNDO* works with my obsessions, such as typography. I have been designing typography for about ten years, since I was in college. It provides a way to bring personality to a project and create a sense of consistency.

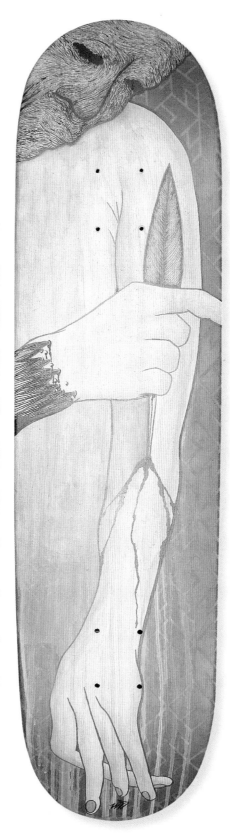

LEFT: "Stand your ground, Fateh Part 03," the skateboard series. Spray paint on wood, 2010.

MIDDLE: "Some days are diamonds, but not today," the Yfel Corvus series. Spray paint and acrylic on wood, 2009.

RIGHT: "Freedom, Fateh Part 03," the skateboard series. Spray paint on wood, 2010.

TOP ROW: "There is still hope for us, Fateh Part 03," the skateboard series. Spray paint on wood, four parts, 2010.

BOTTOM LEFT: Left page: "Devil Town I just loves Daniel Johnston." Right page: sketch for "Family," from the Yfel Corvus series.

BOTTOM MIDDLE: Sketch for "Take one of this with a glass of water, shut up," from the Beginning of the End series.

BOTTOM RIGHT: Sketch for "Come wonder, come wonder with me," from the Yfel Corvus series.

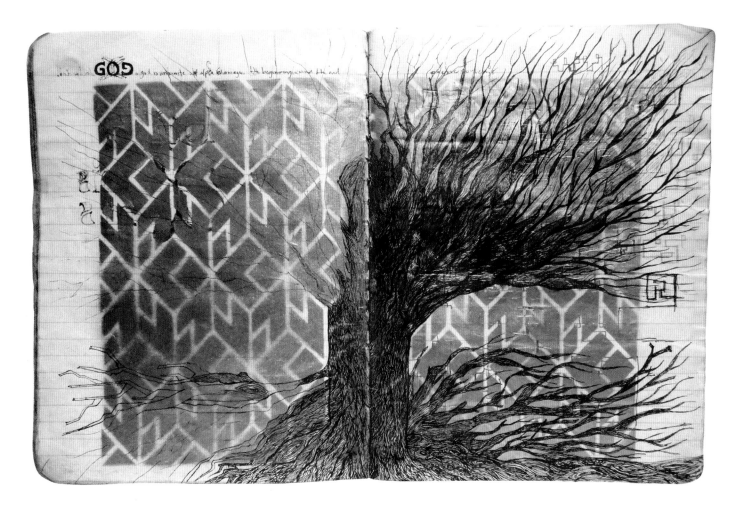

Where do you get your visual ideas?

Thematically, *UNDO* has different "shades." For example, *Obsessive Compulsions* is a series composed of images inspired by Mexican vernacular street imagery, including memories from the local market where my mother used to have a butcher shop, a place full of images. I spent time in my childhood there, and when these images arose spontaneously in my mind I felt the need to draw them. *Fateh* is a series where the key element is the social struggle, the good and bad uses of propaganda. *Yfel Corvus* is a story that began in a recurring dream. I was tired of not being able to see the end of the dream, so I decided to write one.

You have several skateboards under the series called Fateh. What is the meaning behind this term?

In Arabic, *fateh* means blood, and in Hindi, it means victory. Both are essential aspects of politics, the main theme of the series.

I noticed that you work in a limited color palette, which seems to go in an opposite direction when I think about vibrant Mexican street culture. Why do you work with these colors?

I work with four basic colors: black because of its hardness; white for purity; red for blood—another childhood obsession, perhaps born of my mother's

butcher shop; and the most important color for me, gold. I love gold's duality: On the one hand, it represents the divine, but it also symbolizes vile, earthly things such as ambition, avarice, envy, and desire. In other words, gold also symbolizes the "human."

What do you consider your favorite art or design project?

That would be *UNDO*; a place of exploration and experimentation that allows me to deal with my day job. One of the projects I enjoyed most was an installation that was part of the first *UNDO* solo exhibition: "Fateh Exhibit Part 01 Who is really the terrorist?" which consisted of a wooden chair with picks and cow blood. The blood symbolized guilt, and it was fun for me to see how people became stained while walking through, with what they thought was red paint, and thus they shared the "guilt."

Recently, what I enjoy most is to add images to skateboards, for two reasons: the skateboard's intrinsic value as a symbol of rebellion, and when I add images to it, I always remember that the artwork must complement the symbolic value of the object.

As a designer, one of my favorite projects was to design, for five years, *La Mosca en la Pared*

[The Fly on the Wall], an eclectic and experimental rock magazine. This was a laboratory where I had a lot of fun, and it helped me to define many design aspects.

I started as a designer and then realized that I wanted to make art, but I think if I started as an artist I probably would have wanted to become a designer.

Can you name some favorite Mexican or Latin artists or designers that inspire you?

There are several artists and designers whose work I like, but I think now my favorites would be Calma [Stephan Doitschinoff] and Herbert Baglione from Brazil, both great artists.

TOP: Sketch for "G O D" from the Yfel Corvus series.

Anthony Yankovic {INTERVIEW}

ST. PETERSBURG, FLORIDA, U.S.A.

Illustrator Anthony Yankovic's retro-modern and appealing style lends itself well to packaging and apparel design. For example, his 2009 limited-edition packaging for Dentyne chewing gum is now a collector's item. In addition to working with various skate industry companies, his editorial work has appeared in the pages of youth-oriented indie magazines such as *Nylon* and *Anthem*.

Where are you from, and how did you design your first skate deck?

I'm originally from northeast Ohio and I currently live in St. Petersburg, Florida, with my wife, Brooke, and son Julian. I have a bachelor's degree in graphic design from Ohio University. My artwork has been seen on everything from Alien Workshop skateboards and K2 snowboards to a flip-top container of Dentyne gum. My first skateboard graphics were for Sunsports Skateshop in Columbus, Ohio. Eventually, I finagled my way into designing a couple of boards for Ethan Fowler and Foundation Skateboards.

What was the first art piece or artist to influence you?

G.I. Joe comic books and all the late-seventies and eighties Marvel and DC comic books—I would just stare at those covers like a mental case trying to figure out the formula behind their creation. I never quite got it down. I guess that's why I don't draw comics.

ABOVE: Anthony Yankovic. Photo: Brooke Yankovic.

BELOW: Foundation Skateboards, Cruiser deck, 2010.

OPPOSITE PAGE: Embassy Board-shop, Shop deck, 2009.

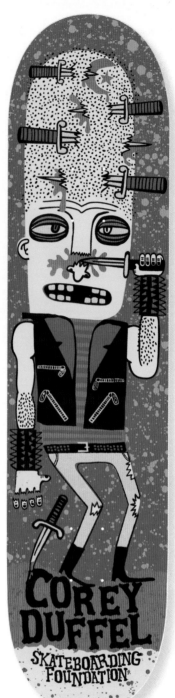

COREY DUFFEL SKATEBOARDING FOUNDATION

ANGEL RAMIREZ SKATEBOARDING FOUNDATION

GARETH STEHR SKATEBOARDING FOUNDATION

SIERRA FELLERS SKATEBOARDING FOUNDATION

TOP ROW, LEFT TO RIGHT:
Foundation Skateboards, Corey Duffel Pro Model, 2009. Foundation Skateboards, Angel Ramirez Pro Model, 2009. Foundation Skateboards, Gareth Stehr Pro Model, 2009. Foundation Skateboards, Sierra Fellers Pro Model, 2009.

LEFT: Alien Workshop, Steve Berra Glugs series, 2007.

OPPOSITE PAGE: "Dickpicker," acrylic and ink on watercolor paper, 22 X 30 inches (56 X 76 cm), 2006.

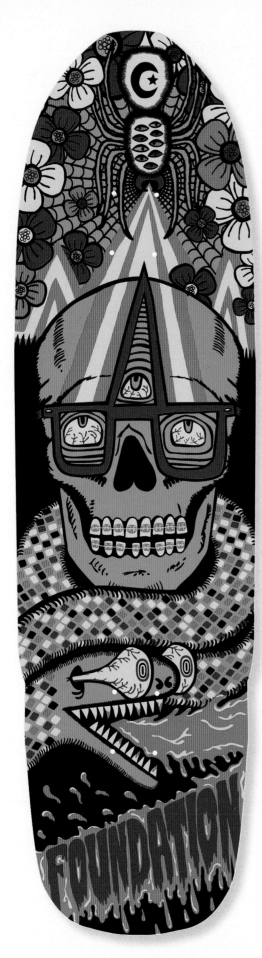

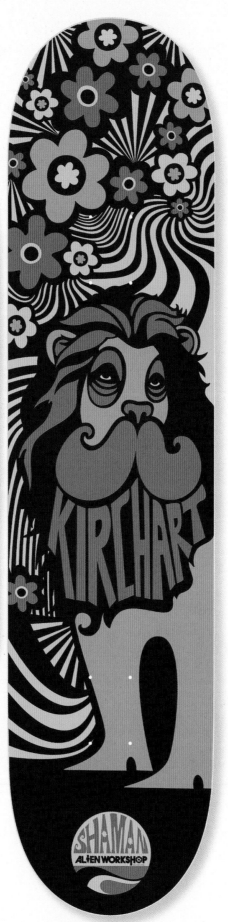

How would you describe your style?

My style is random and varied. I've never stuck to doing one thing over and over again. That being said, there is always a firm link to the past in everything I do.

What or who are your influences?

As far as artwork for skateboards goes, Mike Hill, Sean Cliver, Marc McKee, Jim Phillips, and VCJ. I don't stylistically emulate them, but they are responsible for some of my all-time favorite skateboards.

Where do you get your ideas? Do you create any preparatory drawings for your board designs?

Lately, I've been drawing goofy doodles on paper, scanning them, and then completely disassembling and reassembling them in Illustrator. The final piece may appear to be a character that was drawn off the cuff, but more than likely it has been meticulously labored over to a sickening point.

What are you currently working on?

A pro series for Foundation.

Do you have any collections?

Board collections? Just the ones I've designed. How boring is that?

Describe yourself in five words.

Grumpy, lumpy, and sometimes drunky.

Buying Local 35th North Skateshop

SEATTLE, WASHINGTON, U.S.A.

The first thing you notice about 35th North Skate-shop in Seattle is that it's not on 35th North—the name is taken from a former location. The well-known shop is actually located in the heart of the city, at the intersection of East Pike and 11th Ave. Many skate shops now host gallery shows of artists involved in the skate industry, and 35th North is one such example.

The art space at 35th North Skateshop is a collaboration between the shop and art curator Damion Hayes, former director of BLVD Gallery in Seattle. Hayes has been influential in developing the Seattle area "urban" art scene through producing critically acclaimed exhibitions and promoting acceptance of street art as a legitimate genre in

the art world. By creating a respected art venue that stands apart from traditional art galleries, Hayes has succeeded in building exposure for artists who contribute to the character of the skateboarding community.

Through Hayes's thoughtful curation, 35th North showcases some of the brightest emerging artists from the region, filling a niche as a much-needed gallery in which artists are free to create their work, without the heavy hand of the "market" influencing or directing them. A new artist is featured each month. The artist also designs and illustrates a signature 35th North skateboard deck produced in conjunction with the exhibition, bringing an affordable way to collect art at $35 (£22)

a pop. The shop produces eighty decks split over four sizes. Advertising only happens through Facebook and word of mouth—which is proving to be quite successful, as the boards sell out each month.

TOP: East wall gallery space of 35th North Skateshop featuring the work of artist Junichi Tsuneoka.

UPPER LEFT: 35th North Skateshop is located on the corner of East Pike and 11th Ave. in Seattle.

UPPER MIDDLE: Interior wall space inside shop.

UPPER RIGHT: 35th North employees Jack Jourard and Graham McClure. All Photos by Shogo Ota.

LEFT: Board graphics Nhon Nguyen, 35th North Skateshop U.S.A., 2010.

OPPOSITE FAR LEFT: Board graphics by Michael McGovern, 35th North Skateshop U.S.A., 2010.

OPPOSITE MIDDLE: Board graphics by Junichi Tsuneoka, 35th North Skateshop U.S.A., 2010.

OPPOSITE RIGHT: Board graphics by Iosefatu Sua, 35th North Skateshop U.S.A., 2010.

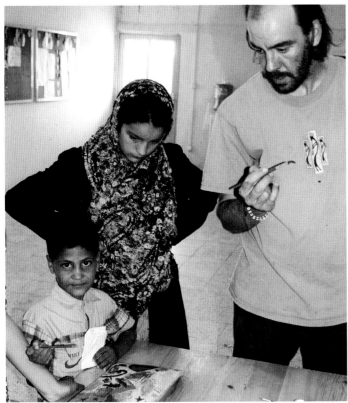

SKATEISTAN
AFGHAN SKATE SCHOOL

Hope on Wheels Skateistan

KABUL, AFGHANISTAN

In Afghanistan, a place of scant opportunity for youthful expression, a nongovernmental organization called Skateistan is spreading the joy of skateboarding culture to a generation of kids surrounded by war and repression. Founded in 2007 by Australian skateboarders Oliver Percovich and Max Henninger, along with Shams Razi and Sharna Nolan, with only three skateboards to share among their students, Skateistan now includes a skate park and educational facility where male and female students learn skateboarding skills, as well as subjects including art, health, information technology, and foreign languages.

The facility has become an escape from the forces of poverty and gender discrimination that have robbed many of the students of much of their youth. Classes offered are particularly empowering for the female participants, allowing them to share ideas and opinions regarding their future role in the development of Afghanistan. These voices are being heard around the globe through Internet and video exchanges with students in Peru, Australia, Germany, and the United States.

Although their situation seems dire, these students embody an amazingly positive spirit for their country's future. The ideas of individualism, confidence, and determination, and the sheer joy of skateboarding, encourage them to move beyond the violence dominating their lives. Skateistan is not simply a skate park but a training facility for future leaders of the country. Students learn not only how to ride a skateboard, but also how to build relationships with one another—skills that can help heal the rifts in Afghan society and end the cycle of violence that has dominated the country for so long.

Son of a Pinstriper Mike Fisher

LOS ANGELES, CALIFORNIA, U.S.A.

Music and pop culture often intertwine in shaping the work of a visual artist, and Los Angeles illustrator Mike Fisher is a prime example of someone whose involvement in music has influenced his graphic style. His creative output is divided between singing with his punk/thrash/death metal band D.I.S. (Drunk in Silverlake) and creating vibrant and edgy graphic designs on skateboards and other surfaces.

Fisher's interest in board sports began at an early age; he picked up his first skateboard at ten years old and soon began customizing them with paint pens. His father was an automotive pinstriper and the family garage was adorned with illustrations such as Ed Roth's Rat Fink hot rod icon and other images from SoCal car culture. Later, influences included the graphic works of Pushead and Marc Rude in *Thrasher* skateboard magazine, and an increasing interest and involvement in the hardcore punk music scene.

After working in the video game industry for several years, Fisher left to join a coworker who had opened Old Star Skateboard Shop in Santa Monica's Dogtown, and was soon illustrating decks for Old Star, Toxic Skate, and Take Out Skateboards. By 1996, as owner of MaximumFlouride Killustration (and later, Wrecking Crew Studios), he began soliciting bands over the Internet for work. Soon, Fisher was creating posters and merchandise for groups such as Slayer, the Misfits, Cattle Decapitation, Motörhead, the Clash, Iron Maiden, and Led

Zeppelin. Although he has several ongoing mainstream corporate clients, Fisher's deepest satisfaction is from the graphic work he provides for various indie bands and record labels.

His work approach is strictly "old school"; he draws skateboard deck images by hand with a Pentel Pocket Brush at full scale. Completed images are scanned into Photoshop where color is added. Avoiding the use of stock fonts, he enjoys customizing and manipulating the typography to enhance and complement his images.

"I love what I am doing," Fisher says. "It is exactly what I have always wanted to be doing. I don't have to commute, I get plenty of time to play Words with Friends on my iPhone, and I get paid to draw skulls and dead things all day."

OPPOSITE PAGE, LEFT:
Mike Fisher singing with band, D.I.S.

OPPOSITE PAGE, RIGHT:
Deck illustration for a promotional giveaway, 2002. Client: Malt Soda Records, a label that specializes in hardcore music.

TOP LEFT: Sketch for "Hella Evil" (part of a series) and final deck for Old Star Skateboard Shop, 2010. This is one of Fisher's favorite decks.

TOP RIGHT: Preliminary sketch and final deck illustration for Take Out Skateboards, 2010.

RIGHT: Pinstripe deck for Old Star Skateboard Shop, 2004. The popular board sold out repeatedly when it was printed in several different deck colors, including wood grain. Fisher learned how to pinstripe from his father and employed those skills here.

From Jozi, with Style Mzwandile Buthelezi

JOHANNESBURG, SOUTH AFRICA

Designer Mzwandile Buthelezi grew up in Soweto, where he developed his unique graffiti-style typography built from his twelve years as a graffiti artist. The graffiti influence is evident in Buthelezi's bold use of type in his design work and in his layered-vector images.

After studying graphic design at the University of Johannesburg, Buthelezi worked in the advertising and branding industry for three years before leaving to pursue his art and develop his design style. Buthelezi runs Satta Design, a small studio specializing in graphic design, illustration, and graffiti art. A solo exhibition is planned for 2011, and he is constantly working toward his lifetime pursuit: to have a graffiti piece in every African country.

Buthelezi's work is inspired by nature, culture, politics, protest poster art, and his favorite album covers. In addition to running his own studio, Buthelezi is the art director for the first black-owned skateboard company in South Africa, Funisu (a Zulu term meaning "the search for a solution"), run by his friend and colleague, Wandile Msomi, a pro skater who rides for DC Shoes SA, Funisu, and Skull Candy. The Funisu logo subtly embodies the meaning of the word through its suggestion that a peaceful heart is "king."

Buthelezi's skateboard designs blend earthtones and iconic African images with bold original typography, projecting a multitude of impressions: modern yet primitive; soft and edgy; altogether fresh, yet still grounded in his native land.

OPPOSITE PAGE: Mzwandile Buthelezi. Photo: Lwazi Hlophe.

TOP: Hacone character board graphic sketch. Client: Funisu Skateboards.

RIGHT: Graff collaboration with KETI. Photo: Mzwandile Buthelezi.

IDENTITY

IDENTITY
"THE VOICE THAT ADDRESSES ITSELF TO
BE HEARD. THE FACE THAT HIDES
ITSELF TO BE SEEN" - IZLIN

FUN1SU

HUMANITY

HUMANITY
GIVE A MAN A FISH,
HE'LL EAT FOR A DAY.
TEACH HIM HOW TO FISH
AND HE'LL EAT FOREVER

FUN1SU

DIVERSITY

DIVERSITY
DIVERSITY IN CULTURE
MAKES THE WORLD
WHOLE

FUN1SU

Beautifully Intricate Hannah Stouffer

LOS ANGELES, CALIFORNIA, U.S.A.

Growing up in Colorado, Los Angeles–based illustrator Hannah Stouffer loved snowboarding. Her perspective today, however, is more of an artist's view. "What I like most about board design is having the graphics printed on a large, tangible object. The surface of a board is a really nice canvas," she relates.

In the past several years, Stouffer has designed snow and skate graphics for companies such as Gnu, Sims, Nike 6.0, Nike Snowboards, Rome, Arbor, Blood is the New Black, and Element. She received her first commission from Gnu in 2006 when an art director she had previously worked with thought her decorative approach would lend itself well to board design. Many of her board graphics begin as gallery pieces. She enjoys how the work most often evolves from personal designs that are modified to fit a board, rather than being created specifically for consumers. However, she admits, "Whenever I design something on a product that is sold, it's always really cool to see it out there."

Although Stouffer's background is in photography and fine arts at San Francisco State University (where she received a bachelor of fine arts degree) and California College of the Arts, she has developed a detail-rich and ornamental style by focusing on her freehand illustration skills.

"Everything I do is fine arts–based and done very traditionally—pen and ink, watercolor, and so on. Everything starts out on paper as opposed to the computer," the artist says.

TOP: "Obsessive Combustion" photo shoot, art directed by and featuring Hannah Stouffer for client Grand Array, is an attempt by Stouffer to re-create an illustration she did previously, titled "Black Roses Tell a Story." Photo by Shaun Pfeifer and Kaisha Shay.

LEFT: Signature series Vans high-tops 2010.

OPPOSITE PAGE: Hannah Stouffer line of decks for Blood Is the New Black and Artsprojekt, created in 2008.

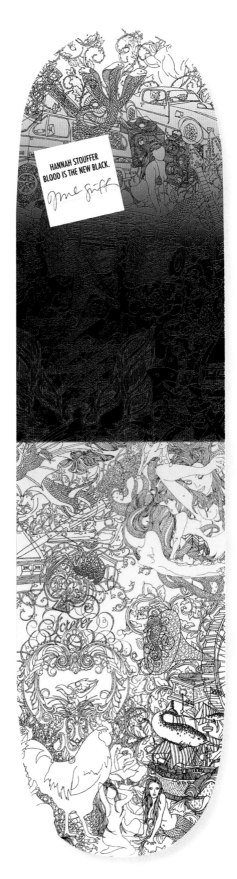

Broken Skateboard Art Haroshi

KATSUSHIKA, TOKYO, JAPAN

Japanese artist Haroshi makes three-dimensional art sculptures from broken and recycled skateboards. He creates his own sculptural medium by laminating stacks of skate decks, one on top of another. Learning through trial and error that not all skate decks are straight or of similar thickness, Haroshi sorts through thousands of used decks and chooses the ones that will stack and laminate properly. After lamination, the stacked decks are cut, shaven, and polished into three-dimensional objects.

This style of carving objects out of separate pieces of wood is similar to the construction techniques used to create traditional wooden Japanese Great Buddhas. In an island nation with a limited supply of trees, 90 percent of all Buddha statues in Japan are carved from separate pieces of wood and then assembled, in order to save expense and material. Unkei (1151–1223), a Japanese sculptor of Buddhas, used this technique and is one of the most popular sculptors among Japanese people today. Unkei would set a crystal called "Shin-gachi-rin" (new moon circle) in the same position as the Buddha's heart, symbolizing the soul of the statue.

Referencing this tradition, Haroshi hides a broken skateboard part within each sculpture, explaining that the part within is meant to "give soul," and is a natural reflection of his spirit and aesthetic as a Japanese artist.

Haroshi's work has been published in magazines worldwide and has been exhibited in Japan, Germany, Malaysia, and the United States.

TOP: Haroshi's studio in Katsushika, Tokyo.

ABOVE: "Thrasher Mario," 2009 using a technique that Haroshi calls "mosaic."

LEFT: Exterior shot of studio.

OPPOSITE PAGE, TOP LEFT: "Apple," 2010.

OPPOSITE PAGE, TOP RIGHT: "Skull," 2009.

OPPOSITE PAGE, BOTTOM LEFT: Piles of recycled skate decks.

OPPOSITE PAGE, BOTTOM MIDDLE: "Cat," 2009.

TOP RIGHT PHOTO: "Screaming Foot," 2010.

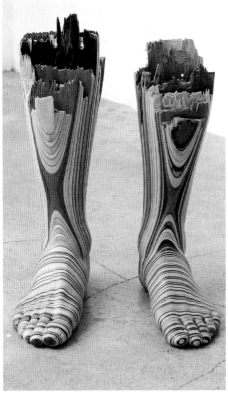

LEFT: Portrait of Aske and a personal deck, 2009.

BOTTOM: Skateboard deck design for Go Ride, 2010.

Love of Letters Aske

MOSCOW, RUSSIA

The 24-year-old Russian graffiti artist and graphic designer known as Aske has successfully moved his art from the streets to the studio. In 2003, he founded Sicksystems, a graffiti crew that gradually evolved into a creative collective. Six years later, Aske struck out on his own, hoping to establish himself as "a graphic artist and not just a graphic designer."

Aske is among a growing group of graffiti-artists-turned-designers. "I decided not to limit myself to graffiti and chose to develop my art through experimenting with different art forms," he says. Aske's street style has attracted high-profile clients such as Nike and Stussy, as well as local companies such as Anteater, a streetwear brand based in St. Petersburg.

For his first skateboard project in 2007, Aske printed his graphics on vinyl and stuck them on blank decks for an exhibition in St. Petersburg. Earlier this year, he was commissioned by Orange Jungle Boardshop in Germany to design a skateboard deck and two T-shirt prints.

Aske approaches board design differently than he does other graphic design projects. "The oblong shape of skateboard decks and snowboards, the position of trucks and bindings, all of these things set certain restrictions on the composition. The shape of the object where the graphic design will appear always influences the final image."

Aske describes his work as "very geometric and inspired by graffiti, constructivism, sci-fi illustrations, and video games." His designs also rely upon letters

and typography. "I believe that my love for letters is hereditary." It's no wonder—his father is a type designer. This love for letters translates well to the board designs. "I think that typographic compositions work really well on decks," he notes.

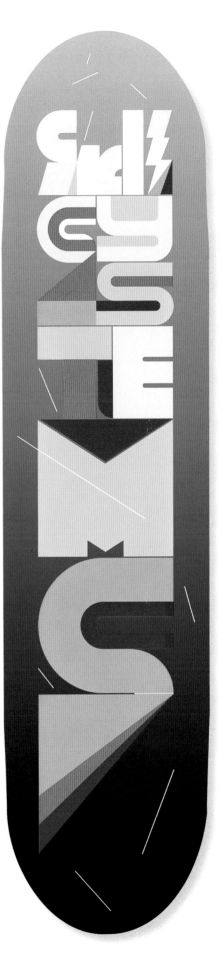

TOP: "Write the Future" sculpture made for Nike global advertising campaign, Moscow, 2010.

BOTTOM LEFT: Silk-screen printed graphics for a limited edition of Anteater Clothing hooded sweatshirts. Anteater is the local streetwear brand from St. Petersburg, Russia.

BOTTOM RIGHT: Silk-screen printed graphics for a limited edition of T-shirts made for the annual Moscow Faces & Laces Street Culture Show by CTRL Clothing, Finland. Stussy, 2010.

FAR RIGHT: Skateboard graphics printed on vinyl and stuck onto a blank deck. Sicksystems Decks, 2007.

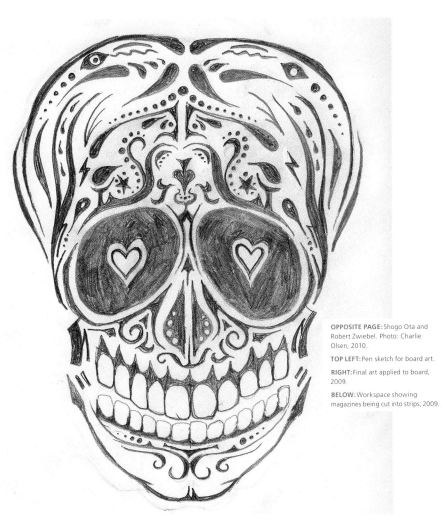

Hung Up Modern Dog Design Co.

SEATTLE, WASHINGTON, U.S.A.

AIGA San Francisco—one of the largest and most active graphic design chapters in the country— invited artists, designers, and skaters to contribute custom skate decks intended for sale in a silent auction. To help celebrate the powerful influence that skate culture has had on design, the institute asked Seattle-based design studio Modern Dog to create and donate a custom skateboard deck for the 2009 AIGA annual fund-raiser, "Hung Up."

Skating and skate culture have played an influential role in the lives of many artists and designers—either directly, through skateboarding itself, or indirectly, through the music and art of skateboarding culture.

To reflect skateboarding's surfing origins, designers Robert Zwiebel and Shogo Ota created a textural collage of colored strips from oceanic imagery. The art on the skateboard deck consists solely of colored strips of grip tape. The deck was then set up with trucks and wheels and roughed up a bit through riding to add authenticity.

The charity event helped raise more than $6,000 (£3,740), part of which was used to support the general and educational programming of the AIGA chapter, including scholarships for college students in the Bay Area.

344 Design
Model 344 Golden Glow-in-the-Dark Skateboard
U.S.A.

Bennet Holzworth
Untitled
USA

Blake Johnson
We Despise
U.S.A.

Blake Johnson
Frivolous Demands
U.S.A.

Blake Johnson
A Dream
U.S.A.

Blake Johnson
Jealousy
U.S.A.

Blake Johnson
Escape into the Fire
U.S.A.

Blake Johnson
Profoundly Sick
USA

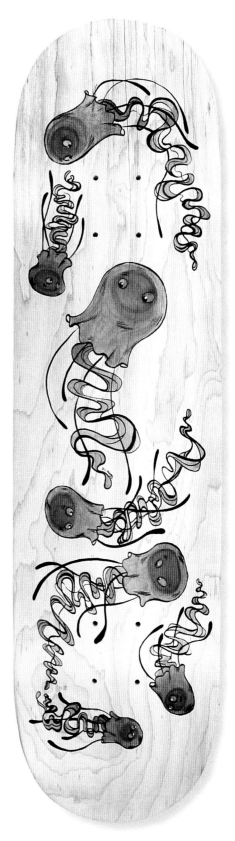

Rad Since 86
Local 77
U.S.A.

Rob Gould
Tutto
U.S.A.

Tim Darragh
Jelly
U.S.A.

Carlos Patino	**Carlos Patino**	**Robynne Raye**	**Casey Harper**	**Mark Helton**	**danamacdesign**
Friday Blanket	*Great White*	*Put a Bird on it*	*Passions Skate*	*Funcie*	*Beast*
New Zealand	**New Zealand**	**U.S.A.**	**U.S.A.**	**U.S.A.**	**U.S.A.**

Carlos Patino	**Carlos Patino**
3D Hands	*Rat Stick*
New Zealand	**New Zealand**

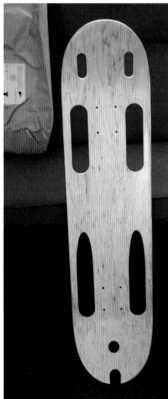

Riverbed Design	**Soldier Design**	**Betsy Walton**
Community	*RAW*	*Tricksters*
U.S.A.	U.S.A.	U.S.A.

Ph.D	**visualism**
Untitled	*B Movie Boards*
U.S.A.	Germany

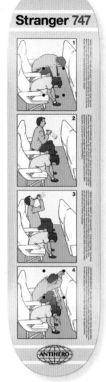

Alan Hynes	**Alan Hynes**	**Alan Hynes**	**Alan Hynes**	**Alan Hynes**	**Alan Hynes**
Freedom Fries	*Airline Stranger*	*Shaaf Specials*	*Rat Trap*	*Hellhound*	*Stranger*
U.S.A.	U.S.A.	U.S.A.	U.S.A.	U.S.A.	U.S.A.

Intermotional, Inc.	**Intermotional, Inc.**	**Hannah Stouffer**	**Darren Pilcher**	**Jeremy Thompson**	**Hans Schellhas**
Brifcore	*Turbo*	*Untitled*	*About Face*	*Robo Skull*	*Meanest Man*
Romania	Romania	U.S.A.	UK	U.S.A.	U.S.A.

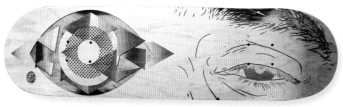

SoupGraphix	StateOfMind
Lindsey	*Searching for a New Place to Hide*
U.S.A.	Greece

Marisa Lehnert	Marisa Lehnert	Marisa Lehnert	Kelly Boyle Designs, LLC	SoupGraphix	SoupGraphix	Studio Sans Nom	Todd Lown
Edicion 12	*Edicion 11*	*Edicion 10*	*Flamingo*	*Garrett Ornateslick*	*Lopez*	*Refill 7*	*Red Bots*
U.S.A.	U.S.A.	U.S.A.	U.S.A.	U.S.A.	U.S.A.	U.S.A.	U.S.A.

Alphabet Arm Design	**Alphabet Arm Design**	**Hot Tomali Communications**	**Tim Benzinger**	**Tim Benzinger**	**Tim Benzinger**
Mr. Lif	*Footballer*	*TV Bars*	*Musically*	*Vinyl Series*	*Established*
U.S.A.	U.S.A.	U.S.A.	U.S.A.	U.S.A.	U.S.A.
Alphabet Arm Design	**Alphabet Arm Design**	**Born Ded**	**Honest Bros**	**Matt Stevens**	**Matt Stevens**
Before and After	*The Crest*	*Sea Section*	*Pattern*	*ML 97*	*ML 97*
U.S.A.	U.S.A.	U.S.A.	U.S.A.	Canada	Canada

Tocayo Design
Mariachi 6
U.S.A.

Tocayo Design
Mariachi 5
U.S.A.

Tocayo Design
Mariachi 1
U.S.A.

Tocayo Design
Senorita
U.S.A.

Tocayo Design
Good Time
U.S.A.

Tocayo Design
Posadas Puppet
U.S.A.

Patrick Carter
Revenge
U.S.A.

Patrick Carter
Salvation
U.S.A.

Marisa Lehnert
Edicion 5
U.S.A.

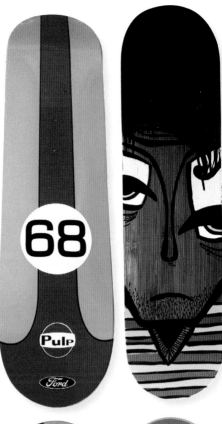

Pulp68
Untitled
Switzerland

Krystie Sargent
Mr. Mellow
Switzerland

Rebel Yell Ltd.
Junkyard
New Zealand

Errandboy
Wonderchild
U.S.A.

Krystie Sargent
Fishface
Switzerland

Rory Doyle
Wasted Skelly
Canada

Paul Brown	Paul Brown	Paul Brown	Paul Brown	Paul Brown	Paul Brown
Wasted Skelly	*Quiet Riot*	*Mumford*	*Eagle*	*Mummy*	*Cole*
U.S.A.	U.S.A.	U.S.A.	U.S.A.	U.S.A.	U.S.A.

Paul Brown	Paul Brown	Paul Brown	Paul Brown	Paul Brown	Paul Brown
Horseman	*Mini*	*Horseman*	*Lopez*	*Rattray*	*Overkill*
U.S.A.	U.S.A.	U.S.A.	U.S.A.	U.S.A.	U.S.A.

Rob Gould
After Ego
U.S.A.

Rob Gould
Luchador
U.S.A.

Rob Gould
Untitled
U.S.A.

Rob Gould
Untitled
U.S.A.

Rob Gould
Untitled
U.S.A.

Rob Gould
Untitled
U.S.A.

SoupGraphix
Rattray Flytrap
U.S.A.

SoupGraphix
Huck 6
U.S.A.

SoupGraphix
Wrapped Up
U.S.A.

SoupGraphix
Pirate
U.S.A.

SoupGraphix
Mr. Peanut
U.S.A.

SoupGraphix
Screaming Girl
U.S.A.

SoupGraphix
Vintage Type
U.S.A.

SoupGraphix
Stabb
U.S.A.

SoupGraphix
Hawk Splats
U.S.A.

Todd Lown
Tuggy
U.S.A.

Todd Lown
Silver Bullet
U.S.A.

Todd Lown
Seattle
U.S.A.

Todd Lown
Garden of Evil
U.S.A.

Todd Lown
Hello Boobies
U.S.A.

Todd Lown
Yellow Submarine
U.S.A.

Todd Lown
Goods Bad
U.S.A.

Tyler Jacobson
Brain
U.S.A.

Tyler Jacobson
I Eat the Legs
U.S.A.

Buero Tiefschwarz
Paco
Germany

Buero Tiefschwarz
Woody
Germany

Tyler Jacobson
Snake
U.S.A.

M-80 Design LLC
Bacon Skate Series
U.S.A.

Wilbor Studio
Abre Caminhos Matriz
Brazil

Wilbor Studio
Da Lama Ao Caos Matriz
Brazil

Wilbor Studio
The Way We Run
Brazil

LEFT: Downtown street to the main beach, Sayulita, Mexico, November 2010. Photo: Joann Arruda.

RIGHT: Murray Walding, Melbourne, Australia, September 1969. Photo: Mrs. Walding.

Surf

I grew up on the shores of Port Phillip Bay, a satin-finished sheet of water with the city of Melbourne spread out around its shores. Apart from the occasional big blow, the bay was surfless and sedate, but it was where I learned to surf and where I learned about California cool. I learned about classic Cali surfboard designs from the American surf magazines that occasionally appeared on our local newsstands. I learned about their bold bands of color and gorgeous pin lines. Their sexed-up appeal was intoxicating for a surf-starved teenager like me.

But fate tragically intervened: By the time I had saved enough money to buy my own board, the world had shifted and anything more than nine feet (2.7 m) long was suddenly uncool. Length, sensuous pin lines, and rainbow nose panels were replaced by short and—considering this was the age of psychedelia—rather plain-looking surfboards, decorated only with flower-power decals.

So, my friends and I decided to add our own personal touches. We gave our boards names. Dave decorated the bottom of his mint green vee bottom with felt-tip pens and named it Peppermint Patty. Tony didn't worry about a name; he just attacked his board with pens and decorated it in artful blue paisleys. Roger named his Winston Charles after a swinging local night club. I carefully painted a large swirl under the nose of my pintail, which read The Holy Ghost.

Everything was do it yourself. The local surf shop on the highway was next door to a panel beater. For a short time, it was a perfect fit. Board after board was sprayed with metallic sparkle-flecked paint—but the colors faded, the glass delaminated, and the shop went broke, and for a while everyone had to make do with the basic color palettes of the short single fin.

All that changed in the early seventies, when Terry Fitzgerald started up his Hot Buttered Surfboards label. His shapes were like esoteric needles more suited to Buck Rogers movies than surfing. Nothing unusual there, but what made Fitzgerald's boards really stand out were the outrageous airbrush sprays created by Martin Worthington.

Worthington's sprays were lysergic riots of waves, planets, and sunsets. A sprayed Hot Buttered board was like owning a Day-Glo surf movie poster, one that you could surf on; but by the time the seventies came to a dreary end, these airbrushed wonders had gone the way of flares, cheesecloth, and moustaches. Hordes of snotty-nosed kids went looking for a new neon consciousness, and they found it in boards covered with the diagonal slashes and color palette of power pop, a consciousness where Echo Beach met sub-6-foot (1.8 m) twin fins. It happened right across the Pacific: Witness the Newport crew in Cali and its Sydney variant, both getting off on the most lurid blocks of color they could find.

Things change quickly. Today's artist–surfer can jump across the ages to summers past and re-create classic sixties designs, or to the DIY aesthetic of the Posca pen, or to the studio artists who can sear your mind with designs that make the board seem like a secondary issue. Except that it isn't—it's still a surfboard and it has to be surfed. Pick an isolated beach break on a hot summer's day, and paddle this surfboard-as-art into the lineup and catch a few waves. Let the mermaids enjoy the view of the bottom of your board, then take it home and clean it up. Stand it up in the corner of your room. And marvel at what this board has just brought you.

Murray Walding
Author of Plastered: The Poster Art of Australian Popular Music *and* Surf-o Rama: Treasures of Australian Surfing.
Noosa Heads, Queensland, Australia.

Martin Worthington {INTERVIEW}

NARRABEEN, AUSTRALIA

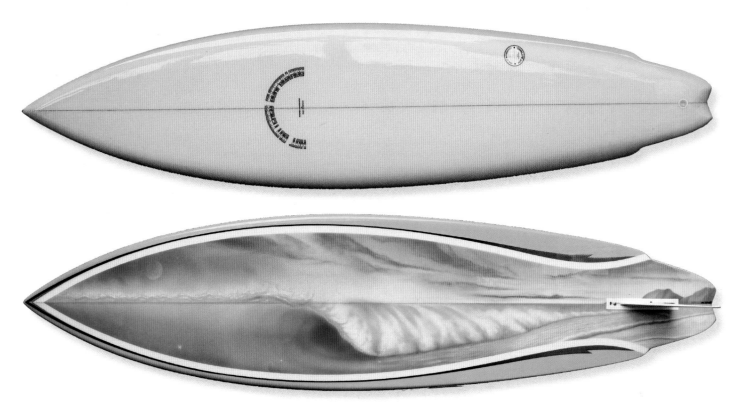

OPPOSITE PAGE: Martin Worthington in his studio. Photo: Mark Onorati.

BELOW: Terry Fitzgerald and his quiver of Hot Buttered surfboards, airbrushed by Martin Worthington. Photo: Jeff Divine.

BOTTOM: The Hot Buttered Surfboards rainbow logo, 1971.

ABOVE: Classic Wing Swallow shaped by Terry Fitzgerald.

ABOVE LOWER: Classic Wing Swallow with Martin Worthington's airbrush art.

Back in the mid-seventies, champion Australian surfer Terry Fitzgerald teamed up with artist Martin Worthington, resulting in the creation of Fitzgerald's Hot Buttered Surfboards, a company whose name was inspired by Isaac Hayes's 1969 album, *Hot Buttered Soul*. The company received immediate attention through the extraordinary airbrush art of Worthington, who pushed surfboard art into a new psychedelic realm. His landscape masterpieces of perfect ocean barrels, leaping dolphins, and neon sunsets helped make Fitzgerald's boards famous. Four decades later, Worthington is considered a true surf art original who helped to define the genre and expand the art form. Worthington's art became as much a part of the Hot Buttered brand as the boards themselves.

How long have you collaborated with Terry Fitzgerald, and how did that relationship develop?

T.F. and I have worked together for forty years. We first met when I read an article in *Tracks* about color on boards, something I had already done on my own boards. I wrote to Terry and then we met and began working together.

How would you describe your trademark style?

Freehand, decorative, surreal, and fluid—I like the art to enhance the board's shape with an emphasis on color and light.

What is your process? Do you make a sketch first, or do you just visualize the results and go for it?

Customers will often supply a picture that they want, or will describe a setting or theme. If I am creating for my own boards, I begin with an outline or concept usually formed in my mind, but as I paint, it develops organically.

Your board airbrush art has a psychedelic feel. From where do you draw your inspiration?

Inspiration is everywhere: the horizon—the play of light in shallow moving water and deep depth; the bush—wind through trees; nature's fluidity in clouds, color, light, the mystery at life's heart.

Do you think surfing and art, specifically board art, are independent of each other?

For me, it's about making art that belongs in or near the ocean—it's certainly not just putting pictures on boards. The art has to belong to the function and lines of the board that help make surfing a rhythmic dance.

How many boards do you estimate you've created?

Too many to accurately count, but in the thousands.

How many boards do you produce in an average month (or year)?

I'm still a production sprayer at Clear Surfboards run by friend Brad Robinson. We make every kind of board with many different designs, which go to many countries, so it is difficult to estimate the number.

Do you ever take special commission work?

Much of my work is custom/commission, usually around ocean themes. I have painted huge paddle boards with sky/sea murals, eagles, whales, turtles, dolphins, rainbow serpents, galaxies, and my own mystical ideas.

Looking back over your incredible body of work, what are you most proud of?

I like to think that my work pleases surfers world-wide. That makes me proud.

Besides surfboards, what other kinds of projects have you done?

I trained after art school to be a set designer and backdrop painter, so mural work has been a natural extension. I have produced murals for houses, hospitals, and public places. I also paint canvases.

With such an impressive body of work, is there a project you are hoping to do some day?

The idea of really painting for myself is still what I want to do, and to have an exhibition, even though the surfboards are everywhere.

If you weren't an artist, what would you do?

Surf more.

Special thanks to Kye Fitzgerald for making this interview a reality.

TOP: Classic Double Wing Pin.
MIDDLE: Area Pin.
BOTTOM: Double Wing Swallow.
OPPOSITE PAGE, LEFT: Slingshot.
OPPOSITE PAGE, RIGHT: Modern Drifta.

Daniel Arsenault {INTERVIEW}

SALT LAKE CITY, UTAH, U.S.A.

Daniel Arsenault studied a variety of artistic disciplines at institutions such as San Francisco Art Institute and Art Center before turning to photography. Through photography, he began to acquire an extensive personal archive of images, which he often assembled into a collage. His collage-intensive surfboard art is a natural extension of his primary vocation. Through his company, Scratt Surfboards, Arsenault designs art and promotional boards for advertising agencies and private individuals.

You have a background as a photographer. How did you make the transition to design and illustration?

Magazines were asking me to do collage, so I just started with photo collage. I made multiple prints in the darkroom and then began cutting and pasting, trying to solve problems. People started to see the collage and it went from there.

How did you get into surfboard design?

The surfboard design began as a way to make some extra money. I grew up in San Diego and was surfing anyway, so I thought I might as well put my designs on surfboards because it's a good canvas to put art on. I did a few and then built a website and started marketing my work. It was a way to get into marketing firms, design firms, and ad agencies. The hard part was getting the art on the boards. We had to use rice paper at first, but then found a laminate that you print on a printer; it's a fabric that will adhere to resin. When I started, the only other person using this process was in Australia. Now it's getting industry wide, which kind of took away the excitement.

When you are starting on a new piece, what is your process?

It starts with photography. I use a lot of graphics and images from the streets and have many images I've collected from around the world while traveling. I'll just shoot stuff on the streets, graffiti, whatever

I see. Wherever I go, I photograph and keep it all. I have a photo archive from walking around Manhattan for two years. I always have the camera with me; looking for anything I believe will work. I like to drive around, get an incognito car that's kind of crappy, and put the equipment in the trunk. Or I sleep in hotels, rent an RV for a few months, and cruise around. On the road, I take photos [for stock agencies], just go around and see stuff. It's fun.

How did you become interested in photography?

I found photography through ceramic sculpture. I learned how to take photos in order to make ceramic decals. I wanted to get some imagery I could put on clay and I had to do it somehow. I got a scholarship and attended the San Francisco Art Institute where I studied sculpture under Richard Shaw, a guy who I really respect. He really inspired me. We began making decals, which was unheard of back then, around 1974–75. Then I got a scholarship to go to the Pasadena Art Center, where I graduated in 1983. From there it just took off. I never stopped.

OPPOSITE PAGE: Self-portrait of designer and photographer Daniel Arsenault.

TOP ROW, LEFT TO RIGHT: Board for Brash Entertainment, 2008. Board for Scratt Surf, 2007–2008. Board for Chris Cote at Transworld Surf, 2006 Scratt Surf, 2007–2008.

BOTTOM ROW:
Scratt Surf, 2007–2008.

How long does it take you to do a surfboard?

If someone sends me the design today, I could get it done in about ten days.

Do you assemble the design in Photoshop?

I like to work in Photoshop because the images that go in there are things that I find on the street. Vector and Illustrator both look too clean for me. When I started doing collage for clients in Los Angeles, I would have to set up five cameras and do multiple exposures. Then I'd go in the darkroom and cut up negatives to get a style that looks kind of edgy. The surfboards looked good with that kind of style. So, I just use Photoshop.

I didn't start this surfboard thing out of something I'd been doing my whole life. It came out of a need to show my artwork. Nobody was really putting great graphics on surfboards, and I felt that there was a market for this. It was a side thing that turned into something kind of nice.

How do you promote your work?

What I like to do is to market the surfboards to ad agencies. I call the marketing department. Marketing people are friendly, whereas art directors will never call you back. If you don't market yourself, you're never going to make it.

Are there any themes that you like to explore in your work?

I've been around a lot of kids lately; it's summer and there are summer art camps, and I've always liked kids' art. In New York one summer, we worked with autistic artists. I love that stuff so much. I'll use it for reference.

I've always been a believer in found objects. The very first photos I ever took were in a junkyard. There is a lot of beauty in junk.

Surf art and culture has been a big deal in my life. When I grew up, I wore white T-shirts, jeans, and desert boots and Pendletons. Everything was surf culture. It's always been a big influence in art and a lot of the art that's coming out has evolved from the surf culture. The first record I bought was the first Beach Boys album. When the surf craze came along, that was the beginning of all the board culture and fashion you have today. The surf thing has had such an effect on everything today. It's a big deal.

OPPOSITE PAGE: Scratt Surf, 2007–2008.

TOP: Daniel Arsenault's studio.

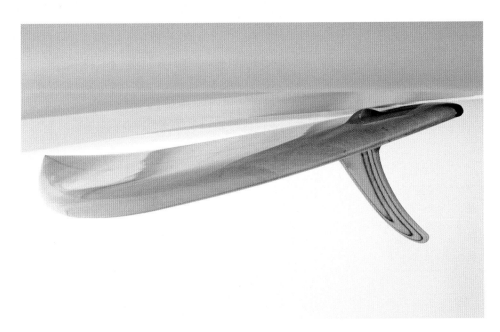

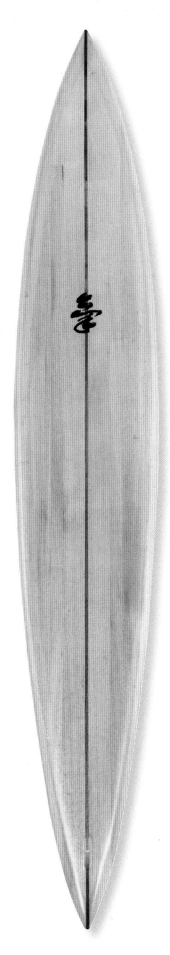

Yoshihiko Kushimoto {INTERVIEW}

KAIHU, TOKUSHIMA, JAPAN

Yoshihiko Kushimoto began surfing at the age of twelve, and by the seventies had become one of the most famous professional surfers in Japan. Kushimoto's design studio is named Ki Surf-boards—Ki meaning "spirit" in Japanese. Influenced by Samurai culture and values and Zen philosophy, his designs reflect concepts of harmony with nature and flow. His boards vary in length from 5 feet, 9 inches (1.7 m) to the 11-foot-plus (3.3 m) Big Gun boards used to ride the big Hawaiian waves.

His passion for surfing combined with a spiritual approach to creating and developing ideas lends a classic look to his surfboard designs.

What do you feel Ki Surfboards creates?

Art, a representation of my spirit.

Your surfboards embody a beautiful, elegant, Japanese-minimalist style. What are the sources or influences of your design approach?

History, but mostly listening to my heart.

How do you get the ideas for your board designs?

My life is about surfing every day, so when I sleep at night good ideas suddenly flash into my mind.

What is your process when creating a surfboard?

I complete the design in my head before I begin; then I shape and laminate the board.

Do you have the design idea when you are shaping the board?

My ideas form while I'm surfing.

You started surfing when you were twelve. What made you decide to shape/design your own surfboards?

Surfing is my entire life, so I decided to make my own boards, just as the Samurai made their own swords.

Do you have international clients? Do you create custom boards for clients?

Yes. Since the 1970s, I have been riding big waves all over the world and have met many wonderful surfers. I've made boards everywhere I have traveled. Wonderful surfers have a great spirit and heart. Riding on the wave is training your spirit.

What is the best way for you to make good designs?

Riding the waves and feeling the energy of nature in my mind and body. To make good designs you must have the right frame of mind. Your spirit condition must be strong, pure, and noble.

How do you spend your time when you are not making surfboards or surfing?

I work outdoors in fine weather, and when it rains, I stay at home and read.

What is the key to your successfully riding and shaping surfboards for so long?

Enjoy the moment.

OPPOSITE PAGE: Yoshihiko Kushimoto selecting a foam surfboard blank. Photo: Takatoshi Okura.

TOP: Ippon Balsa, 11 feet (3.3 m). Photo: Taishi Hirokawa, 2010.

RIGHT: Ippon Balsa, 9 feet, 10 inches (3 m). Photo: Taishi Hirokawa, 2009.

LEFT: Super Fish, 9 feet, 4 inches (2.8 m), 2010. Photo: Takatoshi Okura.

RIGHT: S.U.P. Gun, 11 feet, 4 inches (3.5 m), 2010. Photo: Takatoshi Okura.

OPPOSITE PAGE: A selection of Ki surfboards surrounding the Ki Surfboards logo at Yushima-seidou in Tokyo. Photo: Taishi Hirokawa.

Paul McNeil {INTERVIEW}

BYRON BAY, AUSTRALIA

A native New Zealander, Paul McNeil lives and works in the sleepy surf town of Byron Bay in Northern Australia. A talented and remarkably productive artist, McNeil supplies artwork in a variety of contexts including products, books, brands, labels, and motion work. His iconic surf art, incorporating expressive, crude brushstrokes and a wry sense of humor, has made Sea Surfboards and his current project, Zed, unique and globally distinct.

Describe your role and relationship with Sea Surfboards.

I'm the art guy. Soon after I arrived in Byron Bay, I became friends with Dain Thomas, who had a great little label with his buddy Matt Yeates. We hit it off, and I added my drunken pop sensibilities to the situation.

We opened a gallery/store called Sea Cell and it became the focal point for a lot of gifted slackers. I was sick of seeing white, boring boards, and we were enthusiastic about making a mark. Byron Bay is somewhat the center of surf culture in Australia. The whole town surfs—you get beaten up for not being a Surfie! Life revolves around it, and it's very pleasant. There are a lot of great craftsmen in town, household names in surfing. There's a lot of history here to soak up.

How do you typically go from idea to finished board design? Do you have any work-related habits or rituals that help you get the job done?

Dain and I talk endlessly about all the individual boards and the people we build them for. We ignore all requests (ha!) and just do what we think will be best or whatever we feel at the time. Fortunately, customers seem to like this approach, and we pretty much have carte blanche. We work out every detail of the complete board. I draw the designs out on paper and develop them on my computer. Certain things need to be planned, but on the day of glassing, the procedure becomes rather random. I never like to repeat a design or color scheme. Ultimately, I just want the boards to stand out wherever they are—in the water or on the wall.

TOP: Action shot of resin painting.

MIDDLE: Two Sea Quads on the racks in the room of resin.

BOTTOM: Ari Marcopoulos/Zed collaboration (photo: Ari; resin art: Paul; shape: Dain). One of ten boards that sold for $8,000 (£4,975) each.

Your iconic style incorporates bright colors, simple execution, and handcrafted elements with broad brushstrokes. How did you discover and evolve this style?

I'd been doing boards with regular paint for some time, and soon realized that it would be possible to paint with resins. However, no one did it because it's quite difficult and toxic, and you only have about fifteen minutes to complete the process because of the resin setting. It actually takes two people to do it, and I was fortunate enough to work with Bill McLean, who's probably the best old-school glasser in the country. The tints have such a deep luster, and that's a big part of the overall appeal. But being an artist and designer all my life, I just applied the old tricks of color and balance.

What are you currently working on?

I'm always working on several things. Right now, that includes a new art clothing company I'm involved with, called Art Park; a kids' book; painting; curating shows; and creating more surfboards.

I'm assuming you are a musician because you've also written and illustrated three children's music books. Can you elaborate?

Actually, I'm not a musician or even a frustrated musician! But music is a huge part of my life and I like to surround myself with kick-ass bands. Sea Surfboards is as much about music as it is about surfing. I consider surfboards and guitars to be very similar: Both are fragile, handcrafted, desirable objects that can improve your life until the day you physically can't use them anymore. Consequently, the more well-made ones become more collectible as time goes on. I hope our boards will be savored in the years to come. We put so much love into them that I would hate for them to disappear. I have also written and illustrated a line of Rockin' Alphabet books with my mate Barry Divola. I love them. They are pretty much for adults, but kids dig them, too. So far, there is Metal, Punk, and Country & Western, and by the time you read this, Rap & Hip Hop. I've also started an A to Z of Surfing.

Can you tell us about your twenty-three-year relationship with 100% Mambo, the Australian surf brand?

I'd seen their ads in surf mags when I lived in New Zealand. They were outrageous and cool and I had to work there. When I moved to Australia, I contacted them and have been associated with them ever since. At their height in the nineties, you could draw anything at all for them—totally offensive and funny—and they'd laugh and then pay you

for it! A few weeks later, you would see someone walking down the street with it on their T-shirt. It was excellent! I created my first large range of board graphics with them.

Tell us about your latest venture, Zed Surf.
Zed is our new label. We ended up wanting to get something fresh happening and a little more extreme, just to keep moving forward. Our first board was in collaboration with Ari Marcopoulos, which was a cool way to start the label.

Do you have any personal favorite board graphics? And what about nonsurfboard-related project favorites?
I love the work of Ed "Big Daddy" Roth, and my Fang model was my little fiberglass project that was a tribute to his legacy. The Sea Biscuit is another little honey; I like the Rat-Rod vibe. But I love them all. I'm in the enviable position of doing whatever I want, and combined with Dain's noted shaping talents, we are turning out boards that are completely satisfying—to us at least! As much as they are really hard work, I can't see myself stopping; they are just too much fun to make. I am also very proud of a music video I directed with my buddy Brendan Cook for the American band Smog. They are one of my favorite bands, and to add my art to theirs was a very big compliment. My books, my painting, my dance moves . . . I love them all.

Do you have any role models?
I'm highly motivated by the actions of bands/ musicians The Velvet Underground, Neil Young, and Pavement; surfers Bob McTavish (who continues to inspire with his stoke), Johnny Abegg, Alex Knost, and George Greenough; artists Ed Roth, Mark Gonzales, Keith Haring, David Shrigley, Jackson Pollock, Andy Warhol, Barry McGee, Colin McCahon, Raymond Pettibon . . . The list is endless.

With such an impressive body of work, what would you like to create that you haven't done yet? What does your dream project look like?
It looks something like an insane car, with surfboards on the roof.

TOP ROW, LEFT TO RIGHT:
Spyders Sea Quad, Sammys Sea Quad, Hamish Rat-Quad, Sea Keel stocker, Mad Eric's Sea Quad, James's Pollock Quad.

BOTTOM ROW, LEFT TO RIGHT:
The Lost Sea Quad, Pinky the Sea Quad! Johnny Abegg's daily rider and star of multiple films, Simons DT model, Spotty Sea Stick, DT model JD, Sea Stick.

OPPOSITE PAGE, TOP ROW:
Nine-foot, four-inch (3 m) Sea Horse, one of Paul McNeil's favorites, Aussie colors or Kiwi Ian!, Sea Horse with racing colors.

OPPOSITE PAGE, BOTTOM ROW:
Pugboat art, Sea Quiver: Pugboat, Fang, Munter, and Sea Spoon, The DTZ, a tribute to Jeff Ho/Zepher.

𝕸𝖆𝖈𝖆𝖗𝖗ã𝖔 {INTERVIEW}

SANTOS, SÃO PAULO, BRAZIL

If there is such a thing as an accidental artist, Marcello Macarrão would fit that description. His involvement in surf culture switched from surfboard rider to surfboard artist when a physical injury and rehabilitation period led to his deepening involvement in creating board art. Using themes and images from street culture and graffiti, Macarrão is an artist who uses the surf-board as a canvas for his bold, detailed images, in a style that is always interesting and fresh.

How old were you when you first became interested in surfing?

I was eleven.

When did you start to draw?

I started in 1997.

How did you get involved with surf art?

I began when my friends asked me to paint their surfboard keels, and then, little by little, I started to do art on the surfboard.

How did you find out you had a talent to paint surfboards?

I found out when I was surfing in 2000 and I had an accident that made me unable to walk for about a year; I tore my knee ligament. So, my friend, used to take me to all the competitions and asked me to do art on their surfboards.

How did you come up with your ideas for specific surfboards?

I remember it well. I was at home with my girlfriend and we were thinking about what to do with my white surfboard. My girlfriend said, "Why not do a big painting on your white surfboard?" So, I did an image of Marley; it turned out good, and after that, I improved every day.

When did you get this opportunity?

People in my neighborhood started coming to my house asking me to draw on their boards. Every day, I was doing more and more, and I just loved it.

Talk about your painting technique.

I think I was improving every day using new techniques by importing the best-quality materials. I used to use markers, but today I use spray paint and tints.

Did you do graffiti on something else besides surfboards?

Yes, I did, on walls, helmets, skateboards, a guitar, a Hawaiian canoe and oar, because I always had friends asking me to do it, but I prefer to do it on surfboards and skateboards where I identify myself the most.

How did you develop your technique?

This is a hard question; I guess by learning from my mistakes.

Do you do another type of art?

No, I am dedicated to painting, because it is taking a lot of my time already.

What type of music inspires you to work?

I like Gringo rappers like Jay-Z, Snoop Dogg, and Tupac; I do have a little spot for Brazilian rap, too, like Racionais MCs, D2, MV Bill, and Psy.

OPPOSITE PAGE: Marcello Macarrão with a selection of boards, in Santos.

THIS PAGE: Untitled original board art.

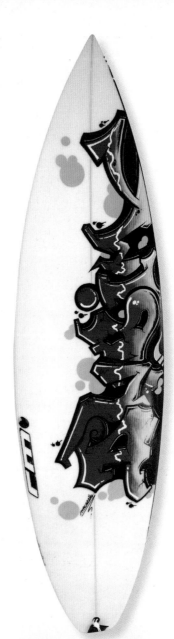
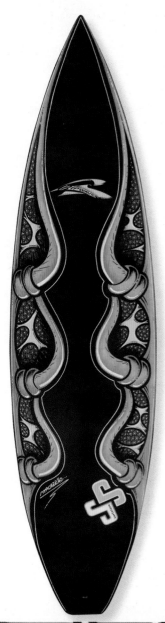

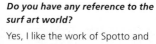

Do you have any reference to the surf art world?

Yes, I like the work of Spotto and Drew Brophy.

How do you see the surfing business in your area?

The surfing business gets bigger every year, and I think the tendency is for it to continue growing.

How and where do you get your inspiration for new art?

I like tattoo designs. I supply myself with recent information by buying books and art magazines. I know it's different from my work, but it does inspire me with new ideas.

Do you have another profession?

Yes; believe it or not, I am a certified plumber! Also, I worked as the manager of a surf store.

Do you have any new projects coming out?

Yes, I have a couple, but I can't talk about them right now. You'll find out really soon.

Are you inspired by any other artists?

The inspiration comes naturally, but I update myself through art magazines, graffiti, and tattoo art.

How can people contact you to create amazing art on their surfboards?

macarraoguaruj@hotmail.com, and I am on Brazilian Orkut network www.orkut.com and Facebook. (13) 78100387 id: 9*9357.

Do you have any relationships with professional surfers?

I am friends with the majority of professional surfers; that's why I'm always present at the surfing contests, and also because I love to be there. They always ask me to create art for the podium. They make me feel at home.

Untitled.
Client: Gilmar Silva.

Board detail

Untitled.
Client: Jean da Silva.

Untitled.
Client: Rasta.

Untitled.
Client: Heitor Pereira.

Untitled.
Client: Danilo Mulinha
(champion longboard
surfer).

Board detail

Untitled. Client: Pablo Paulino
(two-time winner of the ASP
World Junior Title).

Left to right: Marcelo D2 (rapper),
Macarrão, and champion surfer
Picuruta Salazar

Untitled. Client:
Danilo Costa.

Untitled.
Client: Danilo Costa.

TOP AND LEFT: Untitled original
board art.

BOTTOM: Untitled original
surfboard fin art.

Is your graffiti art temporary or permanent? Does using paraffin remove the art? If you don't like a design, can you remove it and make a new one?

The graffiti is permanent until the owner removes it. Using paraffin does not remove the image. The only way you can remove it is by scrubbing it in water with a file.

What materials do you use to paint, and how do you get them?

I use water-based paint pens and spray paint, and I import them from Japan and California.

Besides professional surfers, who are your clients?

I have clients who are beginner surfers as well as veterans. Also, soccer players, the skateboard brothers, doctors, you know, everyone who appreciates good surfing and good art.

TOP ROW: Untitled original board art.

RIGHT: Macarrão at work in Santos.

ABOVE: Rich Harbour shaping one his famous boards at his shop in Seal Beach.

𝕽𝖎𝖈𝖍 𝕳𝖆𝖗𝖇𝖔𝖚𝖗 {INTERVIEW}

SEAL BEACH, CALIFORNIA, U.S.A.

In 1959, a 15-year-old boy named Rich Harbour went into his parents' garage with a saw and a piece of foam and created his first surfboard. Since then, Harbour has crafted more than 30,000 surfboards. Today, vintage Harbours are sought by collectors around the world eager to own a board designed and shaped by one of surfing's greatest living legends. Harbour still works every day, sculpting these exquisitely crafted surfboards in the oldest continuously operating manufacturing shop, at 329 Main Street in Seal Beach, California. After more than fifty years of shaping, Harbour remains a vital influence on the art and design of the modern surfboard.

The design aesthetics of the 1960s boards never look dated. Many would say they are beautiful in their simplicity. Why are the boards so minimal and what influenced this look?

Designs just come from whatever seems to flow with the curves of the board.

When you are shaping a board, do you know beforehand what the graphics will look like or does the design evolve through the shaping process?

I know beforehand. Either a customer has a custom design, or we draw it on the order form.

For readers who are unfamiliar with the actual process of applying a design, logo, or stripe to a board, can you explain this procedure? How has this process changed over the years?

Logos are silkscreened onto rice paper that becomes transparent when placed under fiberglass. In the early years, color was mixed into the resin and brushed over the fiberglass. By the mid-sixties, color was put into the fiberglass coating as either a transparent or an opaque pigment while the board was being glassed. Since the eighties, color has been sprayed onto the foam blank before glassing. In every case, each previous color method was always available, but not always the current fashion.

What is your design process for each board? Do you keep the work in house or do you hire out?

All the designs are in house—color and shape.

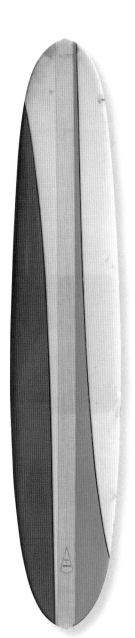

You designed a board in 1965 called Cheater. Why was it called that?

That board had a step deck that reduced the volume of material that had to swing when turning. This also lowered the center of gravity when riding the nose. The board was so good (for the time) that it seemed like "cheating" when you rode it in a contest.

Why did you decide to put black-and-white stripes on the 1963 Banana board?

Rich Chew, who owned the board, designed it with some of my input. This was a recolor of his original Banana board that was yellow with a black center band. It had become worn by the previous season's surfing, but rather than risk getting a new board

TOP ROW:
One of the four balsa/curly redwood boards Harbour sold in 2009 for $10,000 (£6,230).
Harbour surfboard, 1960.
Harbour surfboard, 1961.

LEFT: The Harbour Surfboard logo was designed in 1960 and is still in use today.

ABOVE: Detail photo of Rich Harbour shaping a board.

OPPOSITE PAGE:
Harbour surfboard, 1963.
The first Harbour balsa surfboard, 1962.
The first Banana model, 1963.
The Cheater, 1965.
THIS PAGE:
The Baby Gun, 1968.
The Deep "V," 1968.

that didn't ride as well, we recolored his old one. The board looked so unique that it stood out in contests, making it easy for the judges to identify.

Do you ever take on any custom design work?

No. I was always busy with surfboards, and now I am semiretired.

If there is a definitive Rich Harbour board, which one would you pick, and why?

Last year, I assembled five balsa/curly redwood boards, each made from twenty-one pieces. They were built to commemorate the five decades of my shaping career. They all sold for $10,000 (£6,230) each.

Fads come and go in regard to surf culture and design. Which ones are you glad are gone, and which would you like to see come back?

There are so many shaping fads that have come and gone—too many to list. Color ideas seem to return every fifteen to twenty years.

In the 1970s, you designed custom skateboards for George Powell as well as your own brand of skateboards. Why did the line disappear?

We made a quality product, but insurance costs drove us out of the skateboard industry.

It seems like the company logo has also been around for some time. What year was the Harbour Surfboards logo designed, and who did it?

It was designed in 1960. Before that, the triangle was actually four-sided, like a diamond. I was still making boards in my garage when Ole Surfboards went into business 2 miles (3.2 km) away. He had exactly the same shaped logo, so my brother, who at that time had a graphic design company, straightened the bottom of the diamond and changed the insides of the new triangle to what we have today.

Do you still surf?

I've had some back surgery, which unfortunately prevents me from surfing.

If you were never introduced to surfing—and later, shaping boards—what do you think you would have done for a career?

I was in college trying to become an architect when I quit for the surfboard business.

𝔊𝔲𝔰𝔱𝔞𝔳𝔬 𝔊𝔦𝔩𝔢𝔯 {INTERVIEW}

GUAYAQUIL, ECUADOR

For Gustavo Giler, art is everywhere. In addition to his paintings displayed in traditional art galleries, this prolific Ecuadorian designer creates art on functional objects and surfaces, helping to dissolve the boundaries between art and everyday life. Giler sees the world as his canvas: wall graffiti; temporary body art; hand-painted jeans, jackets, and boots; retail store interiors; tribal-like images on a longboat; and custom graphics on sports equipment, including moto-cross and baseball helmets, and surfboards—lots of surfboards.

Where were you born, and where do you currently live?

I was born in 1964 in Guayaquil, Ecuador, where I currently live. I grew up on a dairy farm where the mix of colors in the country stayed in my mind, surrounded by animals and nature.

When did you first decide to become an artist? Were you raised by artistic parents?

In Ecuador during the long rainy seasons, I learned by myself with books and magazines. First, I started with pencils and watercolors, just getting colors onto paper. I always tried to express myself through colors. My parents were not artists, but they provided me with the materials that allowed me to continue. They worked hard to raise my sisters and me, and when I decided to get into commercial art, it was really hard, but that was my passion.

A few years ago, I visited Ecuadorian painter Leonardo Hidalgo in Miami, and in 2008, his curator, Lenore Stern-Morris, invited me to exhibit my work at Design Center of the Americas (DCOTA) at Dania Beach, Florida. After that event, my dream became a reality.

Who are your artistic influences and why?

Salvador Dali, because he was the subliminal impressionist of all time; Rick Griffin for his posters, album covers, and psychedelic colors; Roger Dean, for his sense of fantasy and because he is an out-of-this-world architect of new visions; Bob Penuelas, because of his cartoons and the way he describes

OPPOSITE PAGE, TOP: Gustavo Giler in his studio. Photo: Manuel Tama, Radical Magazine, 2009.

OPPOSITE PAGE, RIGHT: Giler sketching an idea on a surfboard. Photo: Manuel Tama, *Radical Magazine*, 2009.

THIS PAGE:
Lucky One. Shaper: Mike Michington. Client: Shark Bay Balsa, 2009.
Crabs to the Bone. Shaper: Adam Warden. Client: Shark Bay Balsa, 2010.
All Dogs. Shaper: Adam Warden. Client: Roberto Argenzio, 2010.

the world of surfing through his Wilbur Kookmeyer character; Ecuadorian artist Wolfgang Bloch, for the abstract way he looks at the soul of surfing; Leonardo Hidalgo, for his large formats and the colorful way he presents cultural icons; Stan Lee's fantasy heroes—everybody needs one; Gustave Doré, for his tremendous details and descriptions of characters in monochrome, of natural situations in a fantasy world; Frank Frazetta, for his fantasy, the full colors and great motion; Joaquín Salvador Lavado (Quino), for great cartoons of real-life situations and his sense of humor; and Xavier Portilla, for the colors, geometry, and great proportions of life in every painting.

There are more, but the one that I admire most, and whose creative work I look at every day, is God.

How many surfboards have you created?
More than 300—from simple to really elaborate.

Do you have a favorite surfboard?
The one that I am working on at the time is my favorite.

What kind of tools or paint do you use when you create your surfboard designs?
Posca markers, Sharpies, acrylics, airbrush, spray paint, pencils, whatever is near me at the time I get my hands on the surfboard.

What other kinds of design or illustration work have you done?
Since I graduated from college I have done many—some for advertising agencies, and illustrations and cartoons for the newspaper of the school I attended, the University of Wisconsin.

I noticed a lot of eyeball art on your website and throughout your board graphics. Can you tell us why?
The eye is really important—it represents what your mind doesn't see. We need to be creative to get a mental concept before we see it.

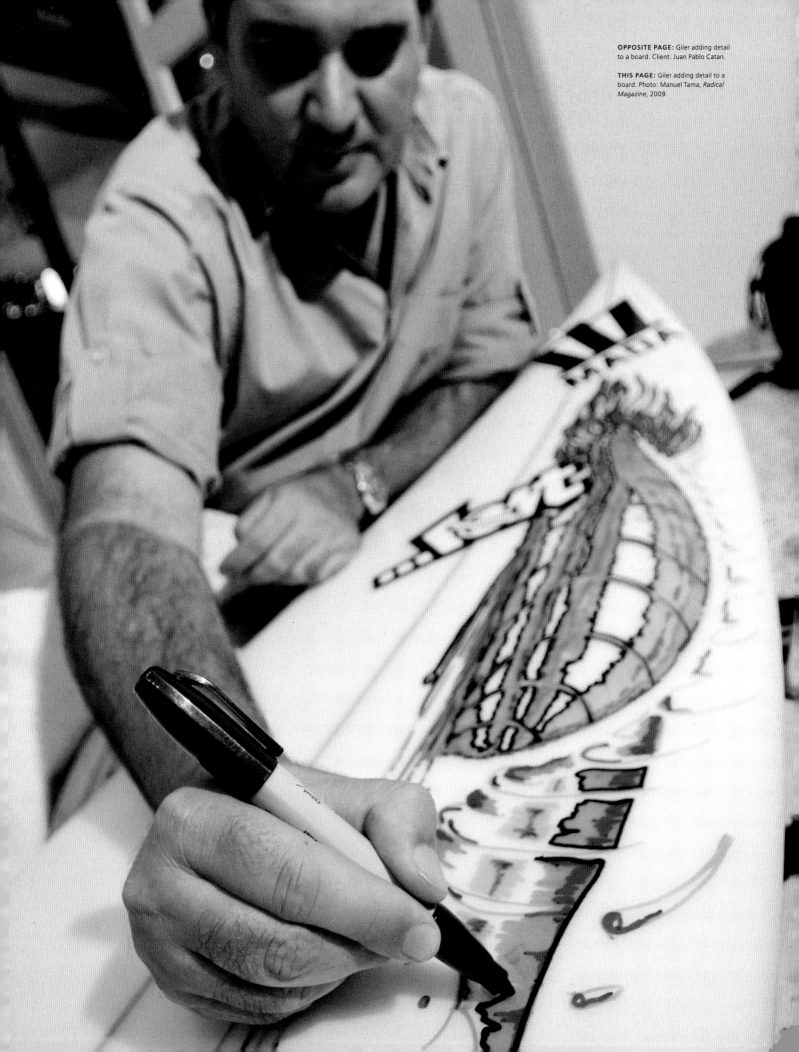

OPPOSITE PAGE: Giler adding detail to a board. Client: Juan Pablo Catan.

THIS PAGE: Giler adding detail to a board. Photo: Manuel Tama, *Radical Magazine*, 2009.

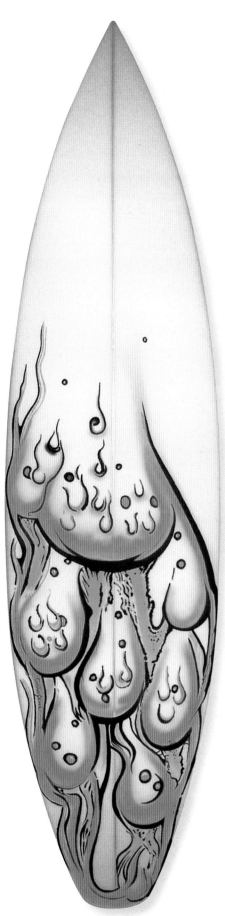

If you could paint a custom surfboard for anyone
in the world, who would you do it for and why?

Greg Noll, "Da Bull," because he was a brave
inspiration for all generations. He has the soul of
a surfer warrior.

Did you paint your own board?

I painted my bodyboard, but just my logos and
some other radical logos.

Have you ever had a close encounter with a shark?

I have seen sharks several times, but they were just
there. I respect their territory, so we just keep them
busy wondering what we are.

Grain Surfboards {INTERVIEW WITH MIKE LAVECCHIA & BRAD ANDERSON}

YORK, MAINE, U.S.A.

Surrounded by quiet, rural farmland and tucked away in the northernmost state of the United States, it's hard to imagine a more unlikely location for a surfboard manufacturer. But Grain Surfboards is unique in other ways as well. Co-owned by Mike LaVecchia and Brad Anderson, Grain's craftsmen build wooden surfboards, using traditional wood-shaping tools and techniques on ecofriendly, locally harvested and sustainable wood. By combining computer-assisted design with old-world craftsmanship and materials, the resultant surfboards are an unusual blend of art and high performance. What is equally unusual is Grain's willingness to pass on this detailed knowledge through surfboard kits and on-site workshops where anyone can learn how to build a wooden surfboard.

You both have boat-building experience. How does that affect your philosophy regarding the shape and design of surfboards?

Mike: Working around traditionally built boats, you're forced to be creative and resourceful. There aren't a lot of resources available to you.

Brad: Our boards are designed in a different way than most surfboard builders employ. With foam, the board is shaped down from a block that is roughly similar in size to the final. The shaper "finds" the shape of the board inside the foam using very fine control of some potentially aggressive tools that require tremendous experience to handle well. Although some simple patterns and scantlings are used, generally speaking, the board is designed as it is being built. Shaping is a small part of building a Grain board because the board is "shaped" using 3-D CAD as a sort of virtual shaping bay before the wood is cut. With this method, the craftsman is building up the entire board from nothing, rather than cutting down a large piece of foam. On an empty shaping stand, little by little, a board grows, slowly becoming a small, graceful

vessel, along with final shaping details added by the board builder (never called a "shaper" in our shop).

How many people do you have working for you? Do you have any plans to expand the company? If not, why?

Brad: Our crew varies a little, but right now, we have seven people working here. Our plan is to create more opportunities for people to surf wood boards and to get the feeling of building their own, along with making our work environment a secure and rewarding place for the people that work with us. The size of our offerings and our workforce is always going to serve those goals. Growth for growth's sake has never been part of our thinking—that sort of logic is a root cause of many global issues that rest on the fantasy of constant growth and the belief that our planet can be perpetually abused.

I'm a big fan of simple and clean logos. Who designed yours?

Mike: The rough concept came about one day when I was doing sketches on a napkin. I love the

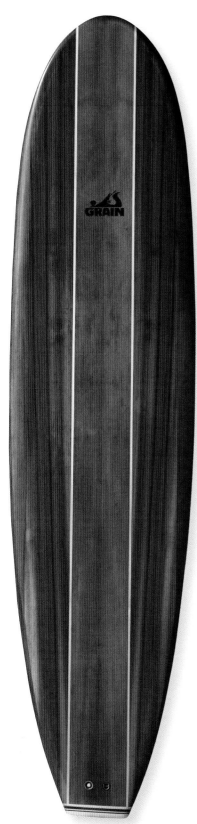

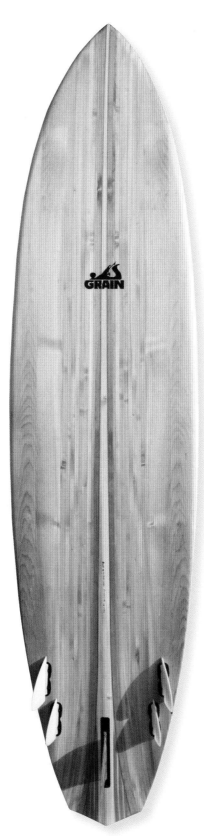
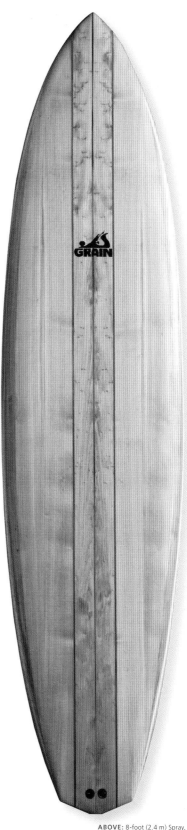

OPPOSITE PAGE, TOP:
Brad Anderson and Mike LaVecchia
in a 1966 Ford Econoline.
Photo: Nick LaVecchia.

OPPOSITE PAGE, BOTTOM:
A rare wood-burned logo. Logo
design by Mike LaVecchia and
Denis Kegler, 2005.

ABOVE: 8-foot (2.4 m)
Steamer, mini-tanker made of
western red
cedar with northern white cedar
detail. Design by John Hamblett,
2009.

ABOVE: 8-foot (2.4 m) Spray, single
to deep-double concave five fin, by
Grain Surfboards. Design assistance
from Malcolm and Duncan Campbell,
2009.

ABOVE: 8-foot (2.4 m) Spray,
northern white cedar with Atlantic
white cedar center planks and
western red cedar detail. Design
by Brad Anderson with Malcolm
and Duncan Campbell, 2009.

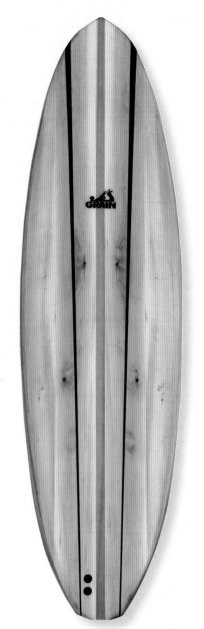

ABOVE: 6-foot, 5-inch (1.9 m) Seed, northern white cedar single-fin with black acrylic paint detail and western red cedar center plank. Design by Randy Gaetano, 2007.

BELOW: August 2010 Grain board-building class, York, Maine

ABOVE: 6-foot, 2-inch (1.8 m) Channel Islands Biscuit, northern white cedar with western red cedar detail. Design by Brad Anderson, 2009.

ABOVE: 5-foot, 10-inch (1.7 m) Waka Fish, northern white cedar with Atlantic white cedar center planks and western red cedar detail. Design by Brad Anderson, 2009.

clean, simple lines of a hand plane, and since that is one of the primary shaping tools we use, it seemed appropriate. I sent the idea to my friend, Denis Kegler, and he finalized it. It's amazing how the subtlest changes can make the defining characteristics of a logo.

What is a typical day like at Grain?

Mike: There aren't many typical days around here. Most of us are here from the early morning until six or seven at night, but there are also plenty of people passing like ships in the night, working until nine o'clock at night or returning after kids are asleep at ten o'clock to get a hot coat on a board.

My day is generally all across the board, answering emails, ordering supplies, building boards, teaching classes, writing blogs, and so on, depending on the day. It keeps things interesting and exciting.

Brad: If I am responsible for any boards that are on deadline, I'll go over to my corner of the shop and get those moved along. I spend a lot of time at my computer, which sits on a desk I made from a 7-foot (2 m) boat transom. We have minimeetings all day long just by swiveling our chairs toward each other. Ten-hour days are common for both of us. Today, there is surf, so I'm doing this interview at home (by the beach), and will surf when the tide drops

after lunch. After that, I'll head to the shop late in the afternoon to prototype a new board-building technique with some of the guys.

How do your board designs and construction differ from other surfboard companies?

Mike: Our boards are unique. We developed our method on our own from day one, and while the core process is the same, it evolves with each board that we build. We start out by designing new shapes in 3-D CAD. Once the shape is dialed in, we create one-dimensional frames that represent the true shape of the board including outline, rocker, bottom contours, and so on. Our boards are as hollow and

lightweight as any wooden board can be, while still retaining all of the strength and structural advantages that wood offers, meaning that they require a very lightweight glass job. All the wood we use is grown in Maine from local family-owned mills. We strive to use the resources as efficiently as possible, and through our creative milling and construction process, we use about a third of the material used in a typical chambered wood board.

Brad: The most notable difference is the wood, as most boards are made of polystyrene or polyurethane foam, but not so obvious is that we use computer-aided design technology to shape our

LEFT: 7-foot, 2-inch (2 m) Longliner, northern white cedar fish with tiger maple veneers and western red cedar detail. Design by John Hamblett, 2008.

boards before they are built, building them around a frame that is precision-cut directly from the resultant plan. Because of this approach, we also differ from other surfboard companies in that we can custom-design a board for a surfer, and include them in the process of "shaping" it. We'll email images of the design, including close-ups of the rails and bottom contours, and the customer can make comments and observations that will ensure they get the shape they want. We have a real dedication to including people in the process of building their own board—they have a chance to weigh in on the design and even to make requests about wood coloring and grain patterns.

We don't have dedicated shapers, sanders, glassers, or polishers. Each board is built by one craftsman who often mills his own wood as well as builds the board and carries it all the way through glass—even, in most cases, packing it for shipment. This nonspecialization makes our boards akin to an art piece personally created by the board builder and through which he's built a personal relationship with the customer. This makes the builder largely responsible for the graphic design of the board, because the most distinctive aesthetic element in the board is the grain patterns that form as the planks meet.

Most surfboard companies are highly secretive about their construction and design process, but you sell kits, offer classes, and teach people your approach. Why do you do this?

Mike: We knew we wanted to offer our designs as kits because we really enjoyed building each board and wanted to offer others the same opportunity. There's a real satisfaction that comes with building your own board that you can't get from buying a board off a rack.

Brad: Sixty years ago, there was no surf industry, and everyone made their own surfboard. Prior to that, every surfboard in the world was made of wood. Those boards were designed to be durable and long lasting and as embodying something spiritual. People are returning to those values as a way to enrich their connection to the sea and surfing.

A lot of people have a hard time imagining what the surf scene is like in a state as far north as Maine. Can you tell us what the vibe is like there?

Mike: There is a small, dedicated community of surfers that live and surf here year round, with all the characters and variety that any other surf town would have. Most of us know each other.

This is a friendly and open place to surf with a mix of old timers and young kids, shortboards, stand-up paddle boarders, and everything in between. Fall is the time if you're a local. Winter can be cold, but when the waves are good and the sun is out, there's no place I'd rather be than out surfing the empty lineups with a couple of close friends.

Brad: In the winter, it's common to wade through the snow to get to the water, so that always lessens the number of surfers in the lineup. That might be part of what makes the scene here a little more chill. The locals can be welcoming and polite because they know they only have to wait it out—winter will come and there'll be empty waves for months.

Cold Surfing, in Style Trina Packard

PORT ANGELES, WASHINGTON, U.S.A.

Trina Packard is a Seattle-born painter and graphic designer currently living in nearby Port Angeles. Aside from a year in Wyoming and a brief stint at Australia's Gold Coast attending the Queensland College of Art (chosen for its surf-friendly location), Packard is a lifelong resident of the Pacific Northwest, graduating from the Cornish College of the Arts with a bachelor's degree in design.

Despite the omnipresence of computers as graphic design tools, Packard has been shifting her interest to handcrafted visual communication. Mainly working with oil paint on canvas, she has recently focused her painting on unconventional surfaces such as surfboards, where the object itself is a source of inspiration. But Packard is a firm believer that adding graphics to an object should not change its primary function.

"Painting a surfboard and hanging it on a wall makes no sense. The best part about art on a surfboard is that you can carry it around and use it. It's not limited to a gallery setting—the board becomes a transportable art piece that is perceived in a variety of ways."

She first surfed in 2000, on a second date. She dumped the guy but quickly fell in love with surfing. Packard's reasons for painting her first board were both artistic and social—the chilly waters of the Pacific Northwest require surfers to wear identical wetsuits, and her newly decorated board provided a distinct visual identity on the waves.

Packard uses water-based Posca paint pens for her board designs. She applies a minimal amount of paint, often using a Q-Tip in the process, adding as

little weight as possible to the board. The result is a soft and subtle color palette.

Her visual influences include Japanese printmaking, Celtic/Norse designs, tattoo art, and the dramatic natural surroundings of the Pacific Northwest. In addition to her graphic work for a website design company, she is in the process of creating artwork for her own clothing line, Val Kyrie.

TOP: Trina Packard somewhere between Port Angeles and the Makah Nation. Photo: Scott Sullivan, 2010.

OPPOSITE PAGE: Board designs, left to right: Broken Tree, Surface. Photo: Scott Sullivan, 2010.

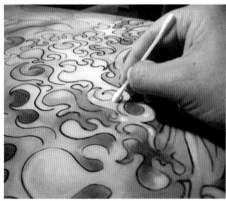

LEFT: Surface (detail). Board shaped by Preston Baggette. Photo: Scott Sullivan, 2010.

ABOVE:

Concept sketch for Surface.

Finished drawing enlarged, tiled, and taped to board prior to transfer.

Rex the cat monitoring progress after completed transfer.

Trina Packard carefully applying pigment to her design. All Photos: Trina Packard.

Design for a Cause Conn Bertish

CAPE TOWN, SOUTH AFRICA

Most artistic surfboards stand the test of time as collector's items, but the board created by South African surfer Conn Bertish lasted about twelve hours. Bertish, creative director at advertising agency JWT, made a surfboard out of ice for a Save Our Seas Foundation auction, an event held December 2009 in conjunction with Cape Town's annual Wavescape Surf Art and Film Festival. Bertish was invited to decorate and contribute a board along with ten other local artists and designers. He explains his choice:

"While other artists, most of them nonsurfers, painted designs and pictures on the board, I wanted the board itself to embody a message that would have relevance and meaning for the sponsors as well as for local and international surfers. I decided

to create a board entirely out of ice, and then document the process of it melting. This would serve as a metaphor for the melting of the polar ice caps due to rising carbon dioxide levels and climate change."

Bertish first made a blank board out of sections of ice, and then shaped it with large support structures that were eventually removed. He shaped the board in a −4°F (−20°C) freezer.

"It was actually quite technical and strangely reminiscent of how the original wooden boards of Hawaii and old redwoods must have been made: first with saws and chisels and then with finer implements to craft the rails and curves. We even used fire as a finishing tool, in the form of a blowtorch. Working in ice was incredible. The lights and shade and reflection were pretty damn beautiful. Cold, but beautiful."

A surfer for more than twenty-five years, Bertish has competed in the Red Bull Big Wave Africa Event five times. Surfing runs in his family—his younger brother won the 2010 Mavericks contest at Half Moon Bay in northern California, and his older brother runs True Blue Surf Travel, the first South African surf travel company.

Bertish's next project—for Greenpeace—is a rideable ice surfboard. "We'll insert oxygen-filled latex balloons into the structure of the board to create more buoyancy, and then freeze a traction pad into the deck and a fin into the tail. We're still experimenting, but it should work."

TOP: Arne Knudson sitting on the porch of his studio in the Hawaii Kai neighborhood of Honolulu.

MIDDLE: Process photos showing the different phases of masking and spraying a Flying Tiger design onto a board. Knudson uses Rust-oleum Specialty Camouflage for a nice flat finish.

BELOW: Flying Tiger series, 2009–2010.

Flying Tigers Arne Knudson

HONOLULU, HAWAII, U.S.A.

As a child growing up in Galveston, Texas, Arne Knudson loved to assemble Flying Tiger model airplanes with his brother. The native Texan learned to surf in the Gulf of Mexico, eventually riding large waves when he moved to Guam after being enticed there by photos from a close friend. After three years in Guam, he moved to Hawaii and earned a graphic design degree in 1992 from the University of Hawaii. While in college, he worked as a surfboard air brusher for Blue Hawaii Surf in Oahu, enabling him to pay off most of his tuition debt.

Today, Knudson lives in Honolulu and works as a graphic designer in a studio behind his home. He continues to paint surfboards, but rather than using an airbrush, he uses cans of spray paint—and the Flying Tiger motif is a design that continues to inspire him.

Painting a typical board takes about three days, including masking and drying time. Knudson achieves a nice, solid, rich color by spraying directly onto the hot coat (resin) before applying a clear coat of lacquer. He enjoys both his work and his work environment: the surf, the sand, the sky. "Technically, I'm 'in a meeting' several times throughout the day," he explains. "[It's] one of the benefits of living in paradise—but don't tell that to my clients!"

Color in Motion Drew Brophy

SAN CLEMENTE, CALIFORNIA, U.S.A.

During twenty years of working as a professional artist, master craftsman, and self-taught artist, Drew Brophy has honed his painting technique through bold designs applied to thousands of surfboards. Brophy lives and works in San Clemente, California, where the beach—and his main source of inspiration, surfing—are always nearby.

To create his designs on the surfboard, Brophy uses Posca markers, the acrylic paint becoming waterproof when dry. "I prefer water-based paint pens over oil-based because they blend more easily and are nontoxic."

Brophy paints directly on top of the fiberglass surface and seals the resultant artwork with a Krylon clear coat matte finish. For boards requiring a glossy finish, he first applies multiple coats of polyurethane, followed by buffing and polishing.

Brophy's surf art, inspired by the work of Rick Griffin and Chris Lundy, has been featured on the Pipeline Masters posters for 2000 and 2004, and has appeared in many magazines, including *Surfer*, *Juxtapoz*, *Longboard*, *Spin*, and *Playboy*. He also filmed a show, *The Paint Shop* with Drew Brophy.

TOP LEFT: Drew Brophy in his studio holding some of his latest creations.

ABOVE: Each project begins with a pencil sketch. Then, working in sections, Brophy paints the lightest colors first, finishing with black outlines and white highlights.

Artwork © Drew Brophy.

LEFT: Guns N Roses, 2008.
Client: Hard Rock Casino, Las Vegas.

MIDDLE: Flying Fish, 2005. Client:
Surfrider Foundation (donation).

RIGHT: Miocean, 2010. Client:
Miocean (donation). Photo: Gary
Zuerker.

Badass Makes Good (Art)

James Victore

BROOKLYN, NEW YORK, U.S.A.

From his start as a wide-eyed teen wanting to make great posters, Brooklyn–based James Victore has achieved resounding success with A-list clients including *Time* magazine, the *New York Times*, Aveda, Moët & Chandon, Target, and Amnesty International. His posters have been chosen for the permanent collections of the Museum of Modern Art, the Palais du Louvre, and the Library of Congress. Not bad for a former dropout of the School of Visual Arts in New York City, a place where Victore currently teaches graphic design.

Although his chosen graphics tool was the ubiquitous Sharpie back when he first started "scribbling dirty words and other provocative drawings across plates and handmade posters," he switched to paint pens, and more recently, Japanese Sumi-e brushes. "I'm doing a job right now and I'm using a Sumi-e brush with India ink precisely because I suck at it. It's so much more interesting than being good at something—I like the idea of chance and mistakes. I can't wait until I'm eighty and have that shaky old-man handwriting." For this self-taught designer who seems to recoil further from computer-based graphics each year, unlearning can be its own kind of growth.

Victore considers himself a "badass," a label he's cultivated for the past decade, feeding into it with provocative work—copulating flies in a condom ad, George W. Bush's face turned into a pirate flag—and happily promoting himself as a guy who says "fuck" a lot, citing Evel Knievel and Johnny Cash flipping Nashville the bird as two major cultural influences. "My heroes have always been cowboys," he says.

Best known as a poster designer, Victore was asked by his mentor, Design Within Reach's CEO, Ray Brunner, to create graphics for a limited edition of surfboards, one of which was donated to the AIGA/NY to help fund their educational programs.

"I made a prototype; they saw it and fell in love. I painted on the first layer and sealed with a second layer. I have a few surfboard blanks I need to finish. Have I surfed? Yes, I'm a solid average!"

Despite his unexceptional surfing skills, Victore is doing quite well on land. His work philosophy may be a key factor of his success, as he explains: "The first rule of being in business for yourself is 'have fun.' I love my job and I take it very seriously. I get to make myself laugh for a living. And if I do a good job, a lot of other folks laugh, too."

LEFT: Peligrosas (Danger! Wet curves, and me with no brakes!). Client: DWR, 2008.

MIDDLE: Smoker, 2007.

RIGHT: James Victore's personal board, 2007.

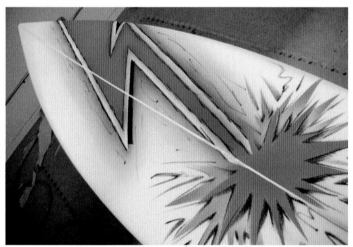

Surf, Paint, Surf Jeannie Chesser

KAIMUKI, HAWAII, U.S.A.

Although Jeannie Chesser describes herself more as a surfer than as an artist, her airbrushing skills make a separate and less modest statement. The fact is, she does both rather well.

Growing up in Miami, Chesser started surfing as a young teen. She won her first surfing contest a year after she started, and continued to excel in competitive surfing. Married in 1967 and widowed three years later, she moved to Hawaii with her infant son for a "new start and in search of more perfect waves," and has lived in Kaimuki since 1973. Chesser has never stopped surfing. She won the 1992 U.S. Amateur Surfing championship at Hawaii's Ala Moana Bowl.

A deep love of surf culture and surfing led Chesser to her first airbrushing job in 1973 for Hawaiian Island Creations. "Except for basic high school courses, I never had any formal training in art. My friend and mentor, Al Dove, showed me how to use an airbrush in the early seventies, and I practiced on my own boards and canvases. I was just kind of pushed into painting my friends' boards, and that snowballed into a real job."

Over the years, her custom designs have appeared on boards by Local Motion, Justice, and Naish, as well as those of top Hawaiian shapers such as Eric Arakawa, Wade Tokoro, and Glenn Minami.

Chesser's idealized seascapes illustrate a perfect understanding of wave shape and motion and her abstract designs symbolize the power and angular forces involved in surfing.

"I do everything by hand the old-school way with pencil, tape, and a razor blade, usually drawing out the design on tracing paper and transferring it onto the board. For other designs, I look at the shaped blank, and 'draw' with the tape. My favorite designs lately are flames and skulls because they are easy but look hard."

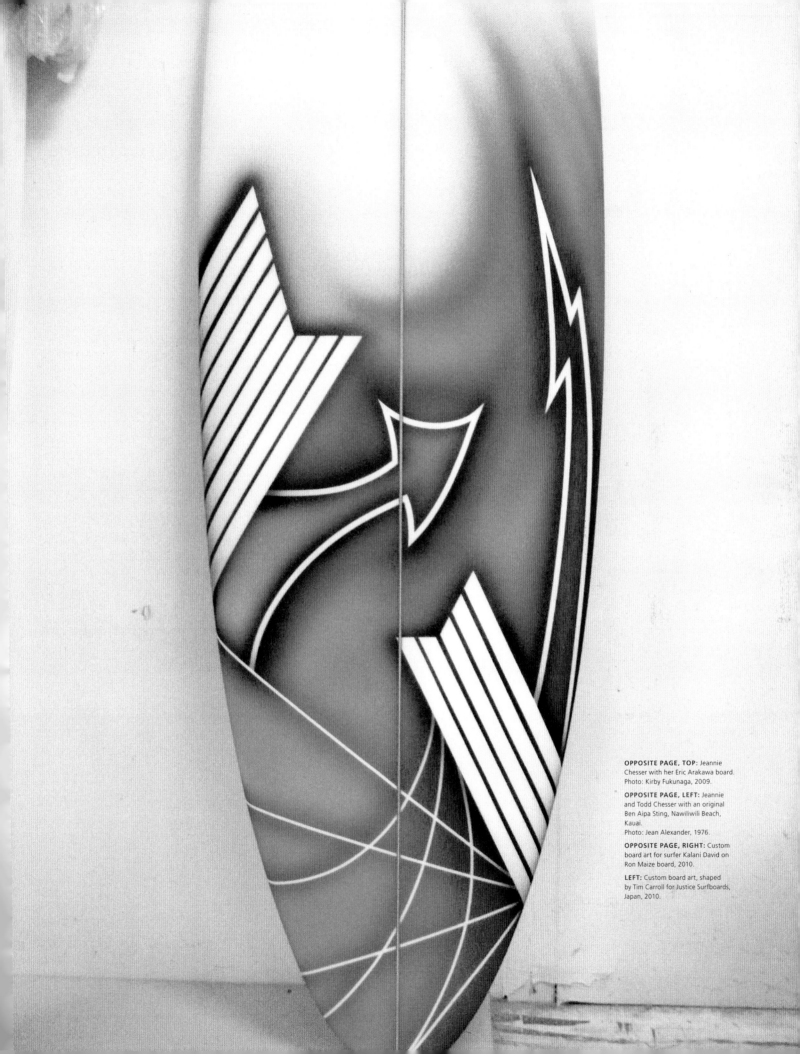

OPPOSITE PAGE, TOP: Jeannie
Chesser with her Eric Arakawa board.
Photo: Kirby Fukunaga, 2009.

OPPOSITE PAGE, LEFT: Jeannie
and Todd Chesser with an original
Ben Aipa Sting, Nawiliwili Beach,
Kauai.
Photo: Jean Alexander, 1976.

OPPOSITE PAGE, RIGHT: Custom
board art for surfer Kalani David on
Ron Maize board, 2010.

LEFT: Custom board art, shaped
by Tim Carroll for Justice Surfboards,
Japan, 2010.

OPPOSITE PAGE: Fame job and skull boards, shaped by Wade Tokoro for Reid Kawamae, Honolulu, 2009.

TOP: Custom board art, shaped by Wade Tokoro for Reid Kawamae, Honolulu, 2010.

LEFT: Airbrush acrylic painting on wood, 2009.

SurfArt Festival Jair Bortoleto

SANTOS, BRAZIL

The small city of Santos, in Brazil, is an unlikely spot to be at the confluence of the global art markets and surf culture, but thanks to photographer and surfer Jair Bortoleto, Santos has hosted one of the largest festivals of surf art in the world.

Though Bortoleto feels there should be no distinction between the art world at large and what is called surf art, all of the fifty artists he exhibited in the Santos SurfArt Festival happened to be surfers. Along with tremendous community support—the mayor of Santos promised a new museum dedicated to surf art—Bortoleto received critical praise for the festival by showing the increasingly global nature of surf culture.

Bortoleto was director of the SurfArt Festival, but recently stepped down due to the intricacies of managing artists and the festival's rapid growth. He now focuses on collaborating with an international group of artist friends. Bortoleto hasn't experienced any difficulties in working with such a diverse group of creative people.

"I only get involved with artists whose work I really admire. And if I feel one of my photographs is a good match with another artist's work, I bring them together. I don't believe in cultural barriers," he notes.

Bortoleto's most recent collaborative project is his own signature model hollow wood surfboard manufactured by Brazilian shaper Felipe Siebert and American designers Dustin Ortiz and Jesse LeDoux.

Growing up as a skateboarder in Brazil, Bortoleto began to capture through his photography the spirit of the people and the culture that surrounded him. As a youth, his hero was pro skateboarder Christian Hosoi, and to this day Bortoleto's work is shaped by images he saw in the imported skateboard magazines.

"In my mind, I always have images in black and white, very grainy, and that's how I remember Christian's images. Grant Brittain has a photo of Christian that really is emblematic to me," Bortoleto explains.

TOP LEFT: Interior shot of the Surf Museum of Santos, Brazil. Photo: Felipe Siebert.

BOTTOM LEFT: Jair Bortoleto, 2010.

TOP RIGHT: Jair Bortoleto's surfboard model for Siebert Surfboards.

MIDDLE RIGHT: Santos SurfArt Festival logo designed by Ben Waters.

BOTTOM RIGHT: Santos Surf Art Museum, 2009. Photo: Jair Bortoleto.

OPPOSITE PAGE: Jesse LeDoux's illustration, a selection from the 2009 Santos SurfArt Festival.

VICIOUS HAT

Riding the Waves with Popsicle Punters Josh Brown

MOUNT MARTHA, VICTORIA, AUSTRALIA

Australian illustrator Josh Brown has been surfing for more than half his life—the 23-year-old grew up in a seaside town on the Mornington Peninsula southeast of Melbourne. "My old man runs his own board-shaping business called Open Cut Surfboards, and he introduced me to surfing at a young age," Brown says. "I've surfed ever since, and I guess it was a natural progression to combine my love for design and art with surfing."

In addition to working as a freelance designer and illustrator, Brown devotes half of his time as senior designer at Australian surf hardware company Balin, where his projects range from print and fashion work to product design and surfboard art. He also creates product packaging, and his work appears in publications such as *Surfing World* magazine.

Brown's style features a lot of collage work, using materials such as old books and objects found in antique stores to create shapes, patterns, and compositions. "From there, I add in my pencil, ink, and watercolor illustrations."

He enjoys shaking things up with a new board project. "It's nice to have something fresh to draw on, and it makes getting a new stick even more exciting!" One of his current favorites is the 5-foot, 9-inch (1.75 m) Oke Popsicle Punter board created for local shaper Rory Oke, depicting a shaka-flashing monster. "Rory has been shaping boards for me for a few years now, and I do board designs for them from time to time," Brown says.

TOP LEFT: Josh Brown in front of a recent wall piece created in 2010. Photo: Robbie Warden.

TOP RIGHT: Illustration for women's clothing label, Folksong Collective, 2010.

LEFT: A well-loved board from Brown's quiver, painted in 2008.

TOP: T-shirt illustration for Australian surf hardware brand, Balin, 2009.

ABOVE: "A Weekend in Sydney," sketchbook illustration, 2009.

ABOVE: "The Explorer," sketchbook
illustration, 2009.

LEFT: Brown's 5-foot, 9-inch (1.75 m) Popsicle Punter, shaped by Rory Oke. Created with acrylic and Posca pens, 2010.

MIDDLE: Brown's 6-foot, 1-inch (1.85 m) shortboard, shaped by Rory Oke, 2010.

RIGHT: 5-foot, 4-inch (1.6 m) Fish, 2010.

Statez of Mind
Wake
U.S.A.

Gerald Moscato & Jane Brown
Trader Joe's Surf Board
U.S.A.

Statez of Mind
Japan
U.S.A.

Statez of Mind
Peacock 1
U.S.A.

Statez of Mind
Peacock 2
U.S.A.

Aloha Studio
Untitled
Greece

Aloha Studio
Untitled
Greece

Aloha Studio
Untitled
Greece

Aloha Studio
Untitled
Greece

Aloha Studio
Untitled
Greece

Andrew Fletcher & Nathan Boyd
Sunday
U.S.A.

Andrew Fletcher & Nathan Boyd
LaLoba • Pony Express • LeNez
U.S.A.

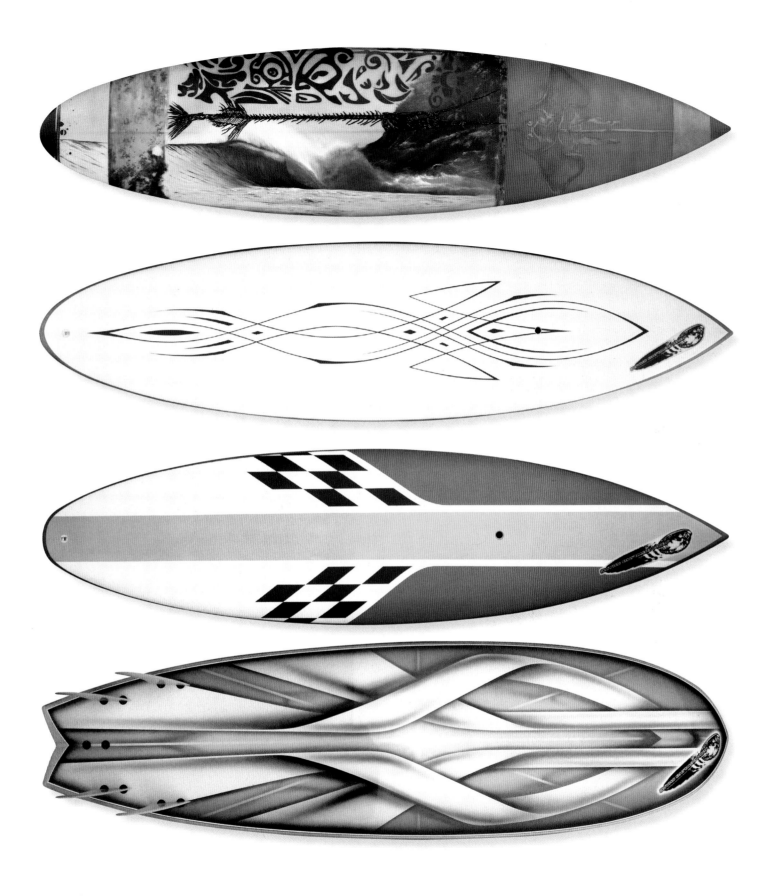

Ashton Howard
Needle Fish Surfboard
U.S.A.

Josh Dowling
Colt 45
Australia

Josh Dowling
Formula One
Australia

Josh Dowling
Space Machine
Australia

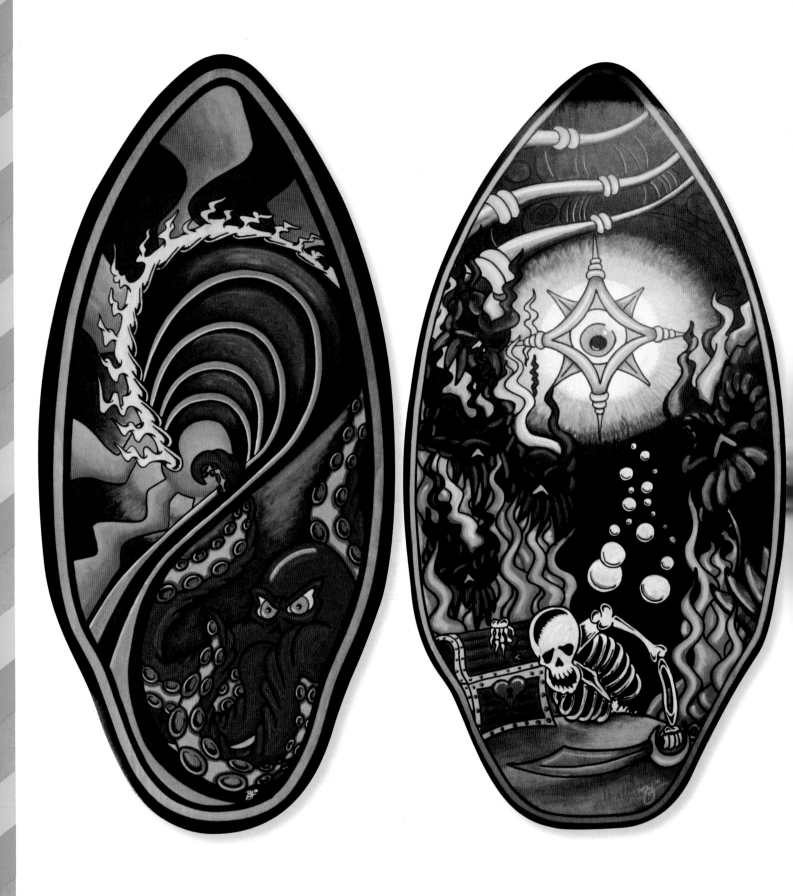

Brian Barden
Oct
U.S.A.

Brian Barden
Pleasure Treasure
U.S.A.

BDOTME
Hooker Victim
U.S.A.

BDOTME
Lovely Victim
U.S.A.

BDOTME
Kill the Dream
U.S.A.

Brown W. Cannon III
Surface Board Collection
U.S.A.

Emil Kozak
Kelly Slater Pro Models
Spain

Scott Patt
9'4" (2.8 m) Kookbox "88" in his art studio
U.S.A.

Art of Style
Jack's Board
U.S.A.

Todd Hansson
Northbridge Surfboard
Australia

Statez of Mind
Erie
U.S.A.

Wade Koniakowsky
Origins 3 5'8"
U.S.A.

Roberto Shapes
1970
Uruguay

Scott Patt
Surf Hex
U.S.A.

Cdaniac Artways
Tribal Blues
U.S.A.

Loslohbros
Flaggsilver Diamond
UK

RIGHT: Matt Barr in Buenos Aires, Argentina. Photo: James McPhail.
OPPOSITE PAGE, LEFT: Untitled, Art and Photo by Daniel Arsenault.

Snow

We snowboarders have always had a complicated relationship with board graphics. In the early days, it was an identity thing. Gaudy, neon-influenced graphics were how we stood apart from skiers and aligned ourselves with our skateboarding and, more commonly, surfing brethren.

But soon, snowboarding exploded in popularity and our culture followed suit, rapidly evolving in many wildly creative and complex ways. Boards and equipment got lighter, cheaper, and stronger, while riders began to express themselves as snowboarders first and foremost. It was a change that was reflected by the graphics of the time, as pros such as Terje Håkonsen, Jamie Lynn (who painted his own graphics), Jeff Brushie, and John Cardiel used their board artwork to showcase their individuality as riders. Graphics helped to spread this organic message to hungry shredders, themselves keen to stake their own claim.

As snowboard technology further evolved, so did the approach to artwork. Advances in technology meant that snowboard artists soon had a range of weapons in their armory not available to surfers or skaters: diecut bases, embossed badges, and laser cuts, among others.

Partly this was to reflect the fact that a snowboard is not as disposable as a skateboard—a snowboard is a significant investment for the average young rider as well as for the company that makes it. Increasingly, the artwork became a way for board brands and companies to get their own messages out there and to make a statement about what they stand for in an increasingly tribal world.

All of this means that in today's snowboarding world, graphics are more important than ever. They are still the primary catalyst for every new board purchase. Compared to those planks of yesteryear, modern snowboards are fiendishly clever compounds of design and technology. Sure, we know these advancements work better and can help you to ride better. But the reality is that most of this technology is under the hood, unseen and, for the most part, not truly understood by the majority of snowboarders. It means that for both parties—company and rider—graphics are usually the way in.

As you pore over the works contained in these pages, you'll discover that today's graphics have attained a level of artistry and creativity that is truly awesome to behold. A little like snowboarding itself? Exactly.

Matt Barr
Journalist and former editor of
White Lines Snowboarding *magazine.*
Brighton, England, UK.

𝕸𝖆𝖝 𝕵𝖊𝖓𝖐𝖊 {INTERVIEW}

**We Are
Endeavor
Snowboard
Design**
Designed in Canada Since 2002

VANCOUVER, BRITISH COLUMBIA, CANADA

Vancouver native Max Jenke grew up snowboarding at Whistler and became a pro rider when he was sixteen years old. By 2002, Jenke and six of his friends cofounded Endeavor Snowboards. As creative director, Jenke researches and outsources talent from all over the world. His energy and vision have earned Endeavor a reputation for consistently creating some of the best board graphics in the industry.

Can you tell us a little about your background and what made you start Endeavor?

I fell in love with snowboarding eighteen years ago, the way people usually do—a friend took me up and I was hooked. I was fortunate enough to turn my passion into a career, snowboarding professionally for five years. During those years, I involved myself with each of the brands, helping to design the boards or outerwear, submitting ideas for ad campaigns, and so on. I also attended university part time to get a business degree, so I knew after I was done with riding, I would find my way into

the industry. In 2001, I had the opportunity to make some snowboards at a factory in Oregon, so I jumped on it and Endeavor was born.

What is your background in design, and how does it play into the development of the Endeavor brand?

I've always been into design and art, and was definitely focused on it in high school. That kind of dropped off for a minute while I was taking the business/university route and focusing on snowboarding. When I started Endeavor, my friend Randy Ross did all of the art under my direction and with my feedback. I still act as creative director, but we don't do a lot of in-house art—most of it is done through our artist network. Everything I do is self-taught, with a lot of help from looking at the right inspiration: magazines, websites, and traveling are all influences. All of that goes into each Endeavor collection and the marketing around it.

Based on the comprehensive designer + artist profiles on the Endeavor website, it is evident

that you are a champion for the people who work with you. How do you go about finding and selecting the artists and designers you work with? Where do you find them?

Our artists are a huge part of our company. Without them, we wouldn't have such great graphics. They are all very talented and at the forefront of the art/design scene. For me, it's amazing seeing what they come up with based on just a brief and some inspiration.

Snowboards are often a difficult canvas to work with, and it's rewarding to hear that on a project we pushed an artist out of their comfort zone. We find artists through all sorts of channels: word of mouth, referrals, Internet, and through them contacting us. We are always looking for new and talented people—Artists Wanted!

Explain the process for creating a board design. As the creative director, do you present ideas and themes, or does the artist/designer have free reign? Can you tell us how long the design process takes from start to finish?

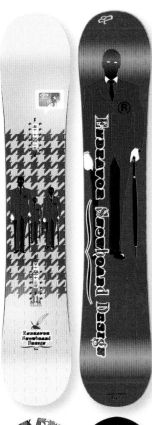

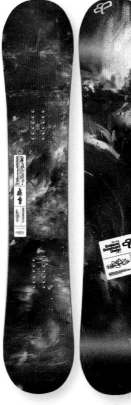

OPPOSITE PAGE: Max Jenke at the Endeavor headquarters. Photo: Scott Serfas.

OPPOSITE PAGE: Endeavor's logo.

TOP ROW, LEFT TO RIGHT:
Sean Coggins Live series; Canada, 2004.
Jeff Hamada High5 series; Canada, 2009.
Mr. Jago Live series; UK, 2010
Randy Ross B.O.D. series; Canada, 2005.

BOTTOM ROW, LEFT TO RIGHT:
Rory Doyle Roots series; Canada, 2009.
Rory Doyle Guerilla series; Canada, 2010.
Rory Doyle Kale Stephens series; Canada, 2009.
Vince Chan Color series; Canada, 2010.
Vince Chan B.O.D. series; Canada, 2010.

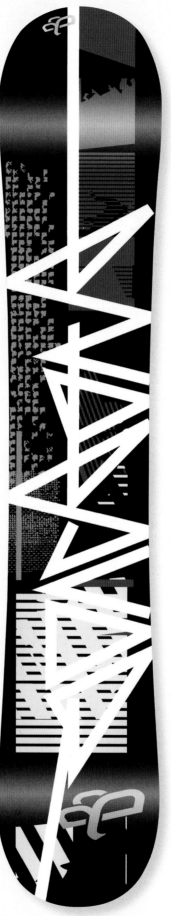

Throughout the year, I gather inspirational material. When it comes to design time for the new collection, I map out each of the different series and see what theme works best for each board/target customer. Often, I will know exactly which artist I want for a particular board. If it's a new design, I generally look around for someone new to do it and expand our network of collaborators. From the theme standpoint, sometimes I have a clear aesthetic, which makes the turnaround really quick. If there isn't really a direction and we leave it up to the artist, the process often takes a bit longer. I guess an average time is about two months.

Once the board design is signed off, what is your involvement with the production process?

We do all of the technical specifications in house. Because of the many years of making boards and working with our factory, we can pull out aesthetic processes that will give the board a bit more appeal. Once the spec is passed on to the factory, we wait for physical samples for sign-off.

Are there any special printing or production effects you've tried? Was it successful (or painful)?

We generally use the standard factory processes, but you can specify the use of these processes. It's always painful getting to the end result when you are pushing the envelope, especially when you work with a factory, as they always want to do what they are comfortable with. But pushing has always gotten us great results, so we are accustomed to the process.

It's obvious there is a lot of talent behind your brand. Have any artists or board designs stood out to you over the years? Why?

There are so many. Randy Ross was certainly incredible, helping me start and grow the brand. He was pretty much doing the entire line, all catalog, marketing, and so on. From there, Marok brought the idea of using fine

FAR LEFT: Thomas "Marok" Marecki Live series; Germany, 2006.

MIDDLE: Thomas "Marok" Marecki Live series; Germany, 2007.

RIGHT: Thomas "Marok" Marecki Live series; Germany, 2009.

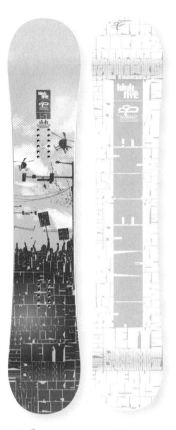

art on a snowboard, shooting his gallery-style canvases and putting them on a board. Rory Doyle and Vince Chan have been very solid for us, and Derek Stenning is the best illustrator I have ever seen.

In regard to board design, do you have any predictions for the visual direction of the sport over the next few years?

As far as trends, it's hard to say. We do graphics far in advance of any industry, such as fashion, so it's not like you can look at what other people are doing. You have to forecast what you think is the next level. Art is opinionated and, to a certain degree, timeless, so for me, it's about coming up with a good concept and following through with a great aesthetic. I still love our boards from eight years ago and think they would sell in today's market. It's also really weird when you walk the trade show floor and you see similar themes on other people's boards—there is always one or two that have come up with something similar.

Which board will you be riding in the 2010–2011 season?

I'll be on the Live 156 and the Next 159 for powder.

TOP ROW, LEFT TO RIGHT:
Nathan Mathews High5 series;
Canada, 2007.
Nathan Mathews High5 series;
Canada, 2006.
Meggs Live series; Australia, 2011
Phunk Studios Diamond series;
Singapore, 2007.

BOTTOM ROW, LEFT TO RIGHT:
Derek Stenning High5 series;
Canada, 2011.
Derek Stenning High5 series;
Canada, 2010.
Derek Stenning Diamond series;
Canada, 2009.
Derek Stenning High5 series;
Canada, 2010.

ABOVE: Katrin Olina, Icelandic graphic artist and illustrator. Photo: Hogni Ingvarsson.

Katrin Olina {INTERVIEW}

REYKJAVÍK, ICELAND

Born in Iceland, Katrin Olina studied industrial design at the E.S.D.I. in Paris before working in the European design studios of Philippe Starck and Ross Lovegrove. Over the course of her career, she has worked as a graphic artist and illustrator in the fields of industrial design, fashion, interiors, print, and animation. As a result, Olina has developed a rich visual language that builds on research, experimentation, and working methods that combine manual illustration with digital manipulation of images. While cultivating a fascination with the natural and the unknown, she has created a personal world populated by fanciful characters, images, and symbols that

appear throughout her diverse work. In 2006, Olina launched a series of limited-edition snowboards and helmets. More recently, she has created the graphics for a new outdoor clothing line by Cintamani, an Icelandic fashion brand.

You were trained as an industrial designer and work in several different design fields. What was it like designing snowboards?

I loved it! I'm always looking for new ways to produce and support my work, and it seemed like a great idea.

Can you tell us more about your work with Cintamani?

Cintamani is building up their line of outdoor wear,

and they asked me to create the graphics for their first snowboarding clothing collection. It was nice to work on a full clothing line, but not all the items are out yet.

The grinning ghost and other characters that appear on your snowboards also appear in a lot of your other work. Can you explain how you've developed these various quirky characters and creatures?

As I work, there are all kinds of characters who come up and introduce themselves. Some of them just pop up effortlessly, and some of them reveal themselves over time.

What I'm trying to do at the moment is build a structure for this world that I am developing. It is

sort of like being an illustrator of natural history, in an imaginary world populated by all of these beings. The appearance of these characters is dictated by their spirits. One could say that the characters are placed along a spectrum of shadow and light. Some of them are dark masses while others are light and translucent, so in a way it's about celebrating diversity. I'm getting to know each character and they are starting to communicate and relate to one another. It's a work in progress.

You reflect a lot on your own creative process and working methods, opening it up to interaction with outside observers, through your own solo shows and various collaborations. Can you explain a little bit more about what this means to you?

We live in an era of unprecedented connectivity. I am totally and utterly inspired by the notion that in the midst of this total explosion of knowledge and global connectivity, we have people who spend time gathering specific knowledge and understanding and translate that knowledge into their personal work. Working with this interconnectivity, sharing, and cocreating are what make the world very interesting to me.

It also reflects the way that I live my life—by refusing to comply with an existing physical structure. My organization is entirely virtual. It is interesting to see how artists actually work today. We are part of a generation that is revolutionizing working methods and structures. I think this really represents the future.

We've talked before about how growing up in Iceland has impacted you as a designer and artist. How has your native country influenced the narratives in your work?

Our creative culture—music, literature, and art—is based on storytelling. Iceland is the place where you look within. We have barren nature and a hostile sea, and this has the automatic effect of causing you to get a little bit dreamy. My artwork also has these kinds of landscapes.

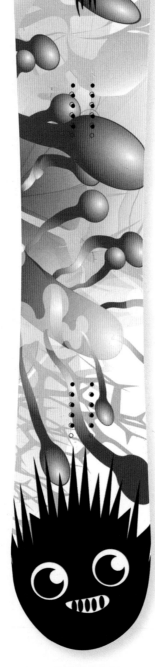

ABOVE: Detail of grinning ghost character featured on snowboard, 2006.

ABOVE: Limited-edition snowboards featuring sublimation and screen-printed graphics by Olina. Manufactured by Elan Colorsurf System (Austria), 2006.

ABOVE: Limited-edition snowboard
by Olina. Manufactured by Elan
Colorsurf System (Austria), 2006.

ABOVE: Close-up of illustrations for
limited-edition snowboard, 2006.

Mervin {INTERVIEW WITH ANNETTE VEIHELMANN, PETE SAARI & MIKE OLSON}

SEQUIM, WASHINGTON, U.S.A.

LEFT: Danny Kass Pro Model board art by Tim "Pinski" Karpinski. Client: Gnu, 2008.

RIGHT: Barrett Christy Pro Model art by Annette Veihelmann. Client: Lib Tech, 2001–2002.

Founded in 1977 by Mike Olson and Pete Saari, Mervin Manufacturing is the last major snow-board factory in the United States. Together, Olson and Saari have transformed the snowboard industry with a mantra of "Build, Ride, Refine," creating numerous innovations in snowboard design and manufacture. The graphics are created by a diverse collective of artists and designers, including Annette Veihelmann, who for the past ten years has been senior graphic designer for Mervin's Lib Tech brand. In this interview, Pete and Annette describe the history and workings of this true American brand.

How did Mervin begin?

Pete: Mervin began in a cosmic vortex of tech-nological madness; aerospace, carbon monoxide whips, custom neoprene, back flips, gold medals, two-part foams, machine shops, skateboards, car jack presses, autoclaves, epoxies, urethanes, losing teams, desperation, inspiration, Cold War Communist threats, powder, icy moguls, and long, empty points.

Where does the name Mervin come from?

Pete: From longtime friend Mervin Winston Leslie III, a northwest surf and skate legend. As soon as our crew learned his real name was Mervin, he was stuck with it.

When did you realize the importance of a strong graphic identity?

Pete: Mike and I were skate kids in the seventies, and we watched skate graphics and the first generation of punk music go through many evolutions. Mike went to a marketing class that gave him some insight. The late-seventies Bobby Burns "the Ski" graphics had been inspiring, as were the eighties Davey Smith punk surf splatter airbrushes. Nick Russian began working for us in the late eighties. Jamie Lynn also brought his art and creativity when he became a rider in the late eighties and took art and riding to another level by the mid-nineties. We always had an open artistic shop. For years, we did custom art, where every board was different and everyone in the shop hand-painted graphics, whether they had art skills or not. Many were so wack, I can't believe we sold them, but we did.

Do you feel there is a Mervin "look?" If so, how would you describe it?

Pete: There isn't really a Mervin look, but we do a lot of hand-drawn or painted rough but colorful artwork. Our graphic application process is unique in the industry and allows us to get bright, vibrant colors on tops and bases through our own twist on the sublimation process. Vibrant, bright, moving, and shade-shifting colors really look good with our process. We drift toward artwork that has vivid colors and contrasts. Gnu has one identity and Lib Tech another. Tim Karpinski sets the tone for Gnu, coordinating with artists around the world and doing some pieces himself. Lib Tech has a crew of artists that we have been working with for decades: Annette Veihelmann, Nick Russian, Mike Parillo, Jamie Lynn, Ryan Davis, Quincy Quigg, Matt French, Carl Smith, Ryno, and others.

How has the graphic identity of Mervin's brands evolved?

Pete: We primarily try to make stuff that stands the test of time, makes us happy, and has solid core elements of some sort: a hint of dark metal combined with some sensitive emo crap, blood, sex, sweaters, and kittens.

Have your efforts to "green" your manufacturing process affected how you create your board graphics?

Pete: We have been a green company for decades. We grew up in the northwest with nature all around us and were influenced by off-the-grid living concepts in the seventies. The seventies gas crisis, Love Canal, and Three Mile Island all happened in our formative years, so the fragility of the planet had been in our face. Another factor was necessity—we didn't have any money, and materials in snowboard widths were hard to come by and needed to be used efficiently. The biggest factor in greening is that we build and do everything ourselves and the factory is right there in our face every day. If something doesn't smell right or makes us dizzy, it probably isn't good, so we don't use it. Most manufacturers have their boards built in an out-of-sight, out-of-mind factory. If there is a toxic process in the manufacturing, they don't know about it, don't care enough to change it, or can't communicate with the factory on a level that will create a change.

The biggest green step we take with graphics is that we sublimate our artwork in house at Mervin with water-based inks, which allows us to recycle the scrap base material. Industry standard is to silkscreen with toxic epoxy-based inks for the bases and automotive-lacquer-based toxic clear coats. The epoxy inks make it so the base material scraps cannot be recycled, and both the automotive lacquer and epoxy inks rely on high VOC thinners that flash off carcinogenic fumes and create a toxic work environment. If your board has a watery thick gloss on it that looks too shiny to be true, it is too good to be true. Minimum wage employees with paper face masks sit in fumes all day and apply the toxic clear coats to feed their families. Companies don't care because they want the "shelf appeal," and decorating boards another way takes time, research, effort, and money. Building anything requires resources and makes a mess of some sort. We try to offer the best, most environmentally friendly solution possible.

Lib Tech has managed to gain a lot of support from the skateboard community. How did you manage to create that crossover appeal?

Pete: Mike and I have always been skateboarders, and the first Lib Tech product was a skateboard, so I think it just comes naturally. We always identified with the early-eighties punk, skate-and-destroy side of skateboarding that is still the heart of skating or good snowboarding today. Our snowboard riders have always been skateboarders who brought that attacking freestyle skate style to the mountains. Lib Tech has been making skateboards for years now. We were one of the first companies to introduce tech skate construction in the late nineties. I think we make the world's most tech skateboard with huge pop and long life. One of our riders, Alex Bland, set the world switch ollie record (over 44 inches [1.1 m]) on a Lib Tech skate. Tap foot for hot ollie action!

TOP ROW, LEFT TO RIGHT:
Travis Rice Pro Model art by Mike Parillo. Client: Lib Tech, 2010–2011. Travis Rice Pro Model art by Mike Parillo. Client: Lib Tech, 2008–2009. Early Release Attack Banana art by Mike Parillo. Client: Lib Tech, 2010–2011.

ABOVE: Original art for early-nineties Emmagator graphic and 2010–2011 Early Release Attack Banana graphic, art by Mike Parillo. Client: Lib Tech, early nineties, 2010–2011.

OPPOSITE PAGE: Original art for Travis Rice's 2006–2007 Pro Model, art by Mike Parillo. Client: Lib Tech, 2006–2007.

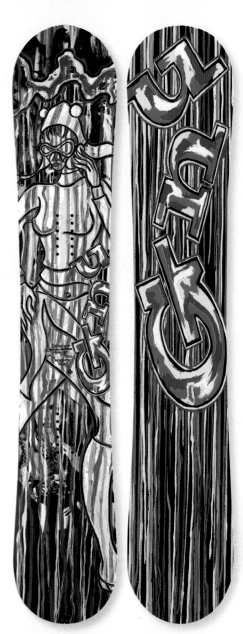

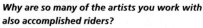

Why are so many of the artists you work with also accomplished riders?

Pete: Nick Russian, Jamie Lynn, and Mike Parillo set the tone for being ripping riders and artists decades ago, and that art element has carried through for years. I think accomplished creative riders want to have art under their feet that inspires them, and are motivated by the opportunity to share their art.

Jamie has always enjoyed decorating his boards, and he has an incredible ability to make a single line tell a huge story. He told me he likes to paint cats because they like to sit around and pose for him, and sometimes, he can get a lady to sit still long enough to do something nice as well.

Parillo was a team rider years ago and developed into an incredible artist. He and Travis Rice live in Jackson Hole, Wyoming, and have done some incredible collaborations in recent years. Nick Russian is a pure artist with an eye for movement and color as well as envelope-pushing content. Matt French is a lifelong skateboarder who is a high-energy creative skater and prolific artist in

every medium imaginable—he can tell you who did what art on which skateboards from then to now.

Annette Veihelmann is another artist–snowboarder that understands the importance of having a snowboard that looks good. After all, it sits in your room until you can use it, and looking badass is important in those sexy lift lines. Carl Smith and Ryno both come from board sports and strong snowboarding backgrounds. I think snowboarder–artists are the ones who see the snowboard as a canvas and are the most inspired to turn them into things of beauty.

Annette, what has been your experience as a female creative in such a male-dominated market?

Annette: It makes me tougher! Guys can be more high maintenance than a PMS-ing girl! Everyone I work with has been super-fun and they don't seem to mind a chick helping with the designs. Plus, I really get to work with a whole variety of people in and outside of Mervin, guys and gals. I love it.

What advice would you give young people interested in designing board graphics?

Annette: The Internet is a great way to get your art out to the world and get noticed. Coffee shop art exhibits are great, too. We have found some awesome potential board art during a latte run. Email us examples of your art! We always love to see beautiful art. But don't get discouraged if nothing gets used. That doesn't mean the art isn't good; it may just not work for the particular year or brand. I've seen some incredible art that just wouldn't work on our boards for various reasons but would look insane on my wall.

TOP ROW, LEFT TO RIGHT:
B-Street art by Nick Russian.
Client: GNU Girls, 2008–2009.

Emmagator art by Nick Russian.
Client: Lib Tech, 1997–1998.

Emma Peel art by Nick Russian.
Client: Lib Tech, 2005–2006.

Emma Peel art by Nick Russian.
Client: Lib Tech, 1997–1998.

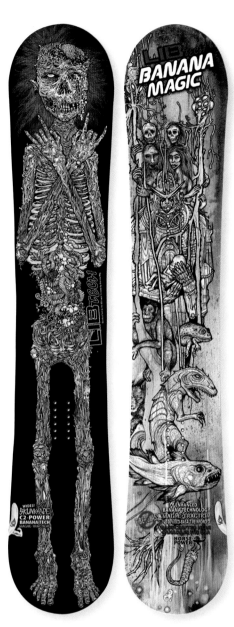

Studying graphic design and graduating with a great portfolio and skill set always helps. And of course, go snowboarding! Surround yourself with people that are into the same things as you; eventually, you'll meet someone that may need your creative skills.

What do you feel has been Mervin's greatest contribution to snowboarding?

Pete: Mike Olson introduced deep carving sidecuts for hardpack in the early eighties, and we were able to ride resorts and faced hardpack, moguls, and ice instead of the powder bliss of hike-only snowboarding. Skiing borrowed that deep sidecut and it changed the entire sport from popsicle sticks to parabolic.

More recently, our Lib Tech experiMENTAL division introduced Banana "rocker between your feet" Technology and Magne-Traction serrated edges, which have been evolutionary steps in snowboard design and made snowboarding much easier for everyone. Prior to Banana Tech and Magne-

Traction, snowboards were misapplying borrowed ski geometries designed years ago around one pressure point per board. Snowboards have two pressure points (feet) inputting control and power into one board to make it work. We are a company founded on change and there is almost no cost for us to try something new, no matter how wacky it is, and we can be on the hill trying a new design in a day. We've been able to lead design change because we are the only ones with a real design kitchen to cook in. Almost everyone else has their boards built thousands of miles away in foreign-language-speaking factories and it costs them much more to experiment.

What mountain would you consider the home Mervin Manufacturing?

Pete: In the old days, it was Ski Acres because they were the only ones who let us ride snowboards on the lifts. Hurricane Ridge is our true home mountain these days; it's thirty minutes from the factory and

TOP ROW, LEFT TO RIGHT:
Skunk Ape art by Quincy Quigg.
Client: Lib Tech, 2010–2011.

Banana Magic art by Quincy Quigg.
Client: Lib Tech, 2010–2011.

Skunk Ape art by Quincy Quigg.
Client: Lib Tech, 2009–2010.

Cygnus X1 art by Quincy Quigg.
Client: Lib Tech, 2008–2009.

ABOVE: Original art for Banana Magic by Quincy Quigg. Client: Lib Tech, 2010–2011.

offers incredible pow and a down-home year-round testing ground.

How did you get involved with designing for snowboards?

Annette: Ironically, I met a lot of the Mervin crew not snowboarding but surfing, while I was still in college studying graphic design. I still had time to doodle and paint and they saw some of my art and liked it, specifically the Cummins family. Matt Cummins was the first to ask if he could use some of my art for his pro model, and then Barrett and Temple followed shortly after. When I graduated from WWU in 2000, Mervin happened to be looking for a graphic designer in Seattle and I got a call from Pete asking if I was interested. I've been geekin' out at Mervin ever since. I feel fortunate that I ended up in the right place at the right time, being able to design within my hobbies, working with people who make me laugh and are into the

same toys I'm into. Working for a company that helps to make the world a better place, through better ecoMOTIONAL products, technology, and fun, is fun.

What are your favorite graphics you have worked on?

Annette: Of my own, the first one I did for Barrett a long time ago, a mosaic made from little squares I cut out of my old surf and snow mags and whatever else I had lying around. It was very tedious and sometimes hard to find the right color, but I loved working on it. These days, I don't have much time to do my own art, but I get to mess with everyone else's art. And our artists are very generous with their flexibility regarding me changing their colors or moving pieces around.

Who and what are your inspirations for your design work?

Annette: Everyone and anything can be inspiring, including sleep deprivation.

Some of our greatest ideas happened on four hours of sleep in a week during catalog production. A warm water surf trip is inspiring. I love surfing and snowboarding; I need it to keep me sane and able to power through twelve-hour days in front of my computer.

TOP ROW, LEFT TO RIGHT:
Jamie Lynn Pro Model art by Jamie Lynn. Client: Lib Tech, 2008–2009.
Jamie Lynn Pro Model art by Jamie Lynn. Client: Lib Tech, 2008–2009.
Jamie Lynn Pro Model art by Jamie Lynn. Client: Lib Tech, 2005–2006.
Jamie Lynn Pro Model art by Jamie Lynn. Client: Lib Tech, 2006–2007.

OPPOSITE PAGE: Original art for Jamie Lynn's Phoenix series pro model by Jamie Lynn. Client: Lib Tech, 2010–2011.

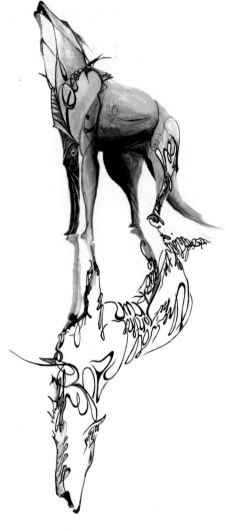

Loslohbros {INTERVIEW with ANDY LOHNER & TOM LOHNER}

LONDON, UK

Andy Lohner and Tom Lohner, brothers born in Graz, Austria, organize their creative output into two streams: commercial and artistic. Their commercial work is done as part of London-based design collective Bubbles & Bones, while their own art is presented under the name Loslohbros. Their commercial graphics appear on snowboard brands including Lamar, LTD, and Sentury. Under the Loslohbros name, they create art pieces using broken boards of all types as blank canvases, such as in their Wild Painting series, an exhibition that recently toured Europe.

When and where did you start Bubbles & Bones? How do you balance your commercial work with more personal, artistic work?

Bubbles & Bones is still quite new, beginning in spring 2009 during a surf trip in Morocco. It was a gathering of designers, filmmakers, and other creative types. We were all old friends who had been working separately but always admired the others' work. It was a happy accident that we often go on surfing or snowboarding trips together. We believe in the same things: to create design that matters for good people, and to learn from each other as much as possible.

We present our personal art under the name Loslohbros, which means that the Lohner brothers have been collaborating in art since 1985. It is nice to have the two styles of work separate, even if they do interfere with each other from time to time.

How do the two of you work together? Do you ever get sick of each other?

We work on our artwork in collaboration and as individuals, depending on the piece of work we are creating. The good part is you can be very honest with your brother, so it might be shocking for observers to see how direct we are in sharing our thoughts during the creative process—but we don't take it personally. Even if we occasionally annoy each other, having your brother as a friend is more like winning the Lotto than a curse.

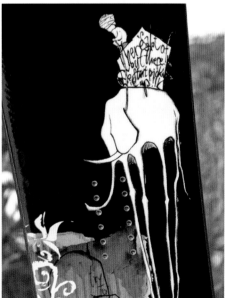

TOP ROW: Lamar Morph base, 2008–2009. Client: Lamar. Lamar Morph top sheet, 2008–2009. Client: Lamar. LTD Sinister top sheet, 2008–2009. Client: LTD Snowboards.

RIGHT: Lamar Morph top sheet (detail), 2008. Client: Lamar.

FAR RIGHT: LTD Sinister top sheet (detail). Client: LTD Snowboards.

What initially prompted you to use a board as a canvas?

It just happened. We had nineteen old, broken boards, and instead of painting each of them, we thought we'd create something bigger. After about nine months, we had completed the Wild Painting series. Creating art on a wrecked snowboard, skateboard, or vinyl is much more exciting than painting on a plain canvas.

Can you describe the Wild Painting series?

The Wild Painting series tells the story of mankind, believing it is stronger than nature, but from time to time nature slaps mankind back. Wild Painting tells us we shouldn't live so wastefully, through

The Wild Painting

OPPOSITE PAGE: Lamar Realm top sheet (detail), 2008/2009. Client: Lamar.

THIS PAGE: The Wild Painting, nineteen wrecked snowboards in one piece of art, 2009.

BOTTOM: The Wild Painting (detail), 2009.

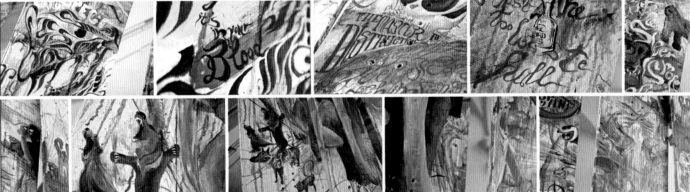

showing the story of nature taking over again. It shows a stampede of animals stepping out of an abstract background that represents the wilderness. The piece was displayed at five shows and events in 2009, beginning in a national art museum in Austria and ending in a gallery in London. Touring with this very large piece almost felt like being on tour with a rock band.

Do you prefer to do commercial boards or artistic boards? Or is each its own kind of adventure?

Both are cool! For client-based work, you have to fit the artwork with the brand, as the interaction with the client is what makes a graphic work. Seeing people ride a board with your graphic or to ride it

yourself sometimes feels a bit unreal—these are really nice things. On the art side, it's good to bring board sports into galleries and show people from the outside how much creativity there is in board culture. Of course, going wild on an artistic board is something that makes you feel absolutely free; it gives you the freedom to rock! All in all, we are really happy to live from our passion. That is something special we don't take for granted.

Do you have a particular approach to a new board design?

For us, a board needs to motivate the rider to go big, smooth—or whatever they want to do. A graphic or shape needs something in it that is

magical, that makes the rider or surfer want to go! This is similar to the surfboard graphics we put onto our own surfboards, the difference being that we create the surfboard shape. In this way, design and board can be even more unified.

Designing a snowboard graphic begins with telling the story of the name of the board. Communicating the style and how it will be ridden mostly starts with sketches, and with thoughts on the placement of the graphics on the nose, the tail, how the base communicates to the top sheet. Next are concept, more sketches, layout, and then, finally, we focus on getting all the details and artwork right.

LEFT: Lamar Ainjel topsheet, 2008–2009.

ABOVE: Lamar Power boots, 2008–2009. Client: Lamar.

TOP: Lamar snowboard binding, 2009. Client: Lamar.

OPPOSITE PAGE: Sidewalls of Lamar Morph, Lamar Endless, Lamar Ainjel, LTD Sinister, Lamar Realm, and LTD Helix. Original artwork on Helix by Sims, Fu, Andi Skant, Harry Brettermeier, Tom Lohner, and Andy Lohner, 2008–2009. Clients: Lamar and LTD Snowboards.

Taro Tamai {INTERVIEW}

NISEKO, HOKKAIDO, JAPAN

Board designer Taro Tamai was born in Tokyo in 1962 and moved to Niseko on the Japanese island of Hokkaido in 1991. Tamai began "snowsurfing" at the age of twelve, and has been hand-shaping his eye-catching Gentemstick boards for more than a decade. Crafted of bamboo/wood cores and bamboo top sheets and sidewalls, with subtle colors and graphics that ironically make them stand out on the slopes, Tamai's boards are renowned for their flexible fins, oversized fish tails, and rideability in almost any snow condition.

As the owner of Gentemstick and as a rider, how would you describe your company?

Gentemstick is a snowboard brand, and it is me. The boards are created from an unframed, freedom-searching mindset. That is Gentemstick.

I am not particularly interested in business. The company is just a way to bring my thoughts into action. I wanted to create something I needed that didn't exist yet in the world. I wanted to focus on the real details of the snowboards.

While extreme snowboarding such as halfpipe gets more attention, not all readers understand the concept of snowsurfing. Can you explain?

Snowsurfing is the original word for explaining everything about current snowboarding culture. Long ago, people used a piece of board for sliding down snow slopes. In the 1970s, surfers began trying to surf on the snow, and from that point on, snowboard culture began to develop.

In the 1990s, snowboarding became an indus-trialized sport and we lost this sense of the unique approach. The media, globalization, and mass production of boards did this . . . now all snow-boards look alike.

Snowsurfing is not imitating the surf style on the snow. Snowsurfing is living with nature's wave-length and achieving the pursuit of enjoyment.

You started snowsurfing at the age of twelve, and began surfing at nineteen. What was the most influential event, figures, or experience in your life?

I learned a lot about nature from fishing when I was a kid. One of my biggest memories is the experience of having pain in my heart from when I saw my natural environment being destroyed.

OPPOSITE PAGE, FAR LEFT: Super Fish graphics: Koji Toyoda.

OPPOSITE PAGE: Impossible, with Par Dahlin at Niseko Gentemstick showroom. Photo: Taro Tamai.

TOP ROW, LEFT TO RIGHT:
Impossible accel camber, Big Mountain series, 2008–2009.

TT Classic flat camber series, 2008–2009.

Trinity accel camber, Big Mountain series, 2010–2011.

TT160 flat camber series, 2010–2011.

LEFT: Kenichi Miyashita tuning up a Gentemstick board at the showroom in Niseko. Photo: Taro Tamai.

TOP: Gentemstick's traditional Japanese small factory. Photo: Taro Tamai.

OPPOSITE PAGE: Supershort snow-surf board lineup.

When I found out the world was big, I met many people who inspired me to keep riding on great waves and snow. Every second of these good moments has influenced me.

What made you move your hobby into a business?

Pursuit of professionalism. Searching for something I love, so I experience no boundary between hobby and business.

Please tell us about your design process.

There are a bunch of ways to do it. Sometimes, I start by using Illustrator, but my favorite approach is to make concept boards from an original piece of wood because the board shape is everything for me.

You have made many boards with no design or illustrations. What is the reason?

For my boards, everything is about shape. You have to really look to see the small logo on my boards. My concept is to express myself and my riding style through these board shapes.

You have an interestingly shaped board called a Double Pin Tail. What is the relationship between the board shape and design?

It's not only about design or shape, but the beauty of the functionality. I think that if a design can show the essence of the function, the board will be a beautiful functional object.

When you test-rode the TT model for your first time in Cypress, Vancouver, you got disqualified for "overspeed." Can you explain?

We knew it was going to happen. Everything was in slow motion . . . I was young and crazy.

How important are the board graphics?

I think they are really important. Ferrari is not just a piece of metal. The true value is always in something you can't see at first. Gentemstick is known as having no graphics and logo, but actually, I spend a lot of time on the small logo on my boards. Conspicuous logos are irrelevant to the true beauty of a board—they are a threat.

What takes a long time is picking the colors, because this quality is key for me. The process of mixing colors for the various boards can take years.

What has inspired you when you design?

All of my inspirations are from the sea and the mountains. They are a gift from Mother Nature.

How is Gentemstick evolving as far as shaping and designing?

Our designs will keep developing in any direction as long as my friends and I continue to look for some-thing better. In 1990, we made a bottom design called accel camber, and Burton started to use the same idea called S-camber around 2008. Also, the conditions of the snow the past twenty years have changed the designs.

You made one board in fall 1998 from sketches you made in the eighties. Why did it take so long?

Actually, I released it in the early nineties, but the snowboard market was a different world and people didn't even look at it. You need to know the right time to do anything, even though you have great ideas.

What do you want to focus on now?

The snowboard world needs to mature in riding, in the snowboarding image itself, in the equipment; everything. All I can do is ride as much as possible and keep making better boards.

Building a successful business from a hobby is difficult, but you did it. What is your advice for young designers?

Be thorough in everything you love to do. Have a dream. Don't give up. Don't copy anyone. Even if you think you can't do it now, try to learn how by spending time with someone who is doing what you want to do.

𝕵𝖆𝖗𝖎 𝕾𝖆𝖑𝖔 {INTERVIEW}

HELSINKI, FINLAND

Jari Salo has been designing snowboard graphics since 1998. An avid snowboarder, this Finnish graphic designer has created boards for pro riders such as Joni Mäkinen and Jussi Oksanen, who represented Finland in the Nagano Olympics. In addition to his freelance work for brands such as Capita and Burton, Salo is also an art director for *Slammer*, a Finnish snowboard magazine.

Can you elaborate on the Finnish snowboard scene? Are you a boarder yourself?

I've been snowboarding since the late eighties. The riding scene in Finland is quite small, and because the resorts are small, it's easy to get to know the other riders. My home "mountain," Talma, is only 55 meters (180 ft) high, and I've had a season pass there for more than fifteen years. We don't get as much snow as you might think—there is almost never any powder in southern Finland, even though Helsinki is about as north as Anchorage. Last winter was amazing here, but most of the time, I was riding in Switzerland, so I missed all the fun at home.

I try to ride as much as possible. In the past five years, I've ridden more than a hundred days a year. I love riding powder, so to get my fix I try to travel every year to Utah or Japan or to the Alps.

How did you get into snowboard design, and how long have you been doing it? What was your first commission?

My friends have always been better riders than me, so when they started to get sponsorships from abroad, they hooked me up with their sponsors to do their graphics. I did my first board in 1998 for Joyride; it was Joni Mäkinen's pro model. Joni is the only rider I know who has had the same theme in all of his pro models. He always has three spruces somewhere on his board. Without Joni's and Jussi Oksanen's help and connections, I would probably have never been able to get such great clients.

Jussi saw Joni's graphics and wanted me to work for him, too. I did all of Jussi's Burton pro models. We try to do fresh things every year, but also to have some continuity in style. My working style is always collaborative. We bounce ideas back

and forth a lot until we are both happy with the end result.

Finland is known for its strong graphic design tradition. Do you find yourself influenced by this, or is the typical Nordic minimalism not a factor in your snowboard designs?

Finland has had great architects and designers. I really love the work of Eero Aarnio, Eero Saarinen, Yrjö Kukkapuro, and Matti Suuronen, to name a few. Those were the old masters. The Finnish architecture scene is pretty uninspiring. Today, there are some great graphic designers and illustrators such as Klaus Haapaniemi and Kustaa Saksi. Nordic minimalism is nice, but there's a fine line between being minimalistic and boring. You can do great minimalistic stuff on snowboards, like Taro Tamai does. But in that case, you have to control the materials and shapes. Designing snowboard graphics where materials and shapes are given factors—it's difficult to play with minimalism without being boring. I don't feel that there's a big influence of Nordic design in my board graphics.

ABOVE: HEAD Snowboards, 2008. This board model is, the Transit, and it features members of Finnish rider Jukka Erätuli's family embedded in vintage photos.

ABOVE: HEAD Snowboards, 2008.

ABOVE: Option Snowboards, 2006. Pro model for Finnish rider Joni Mäkinen.

ABOVE: Option Snowboards, 2006. Pro model for Finnish rider Joni Mäkinen.

TOP: Burton Snowboards, 2009. Limited-edition model.

BOTTOM: Burton Snowboards, 2009. Close-up of limited-edition model, Con-Dominant.

TOP: Burton Snowboards, 2010. Pro model for Finnish rider Jussi Oksanen.

BOTTOM: Burton Snowboards, 2010. Close-up of pro model for Finnish rider Jussi Oksanen.

RIGHT: Burton Snowboards, 2009.

ABOVE: Burton Snowboards. Jari Salo working on pro model for Jussi Oksanen.

LOWER: Detail of design process for Jussi Oksanen pro model.

TOP LEFT: Option Snowboards, 2007. Pro model for Joni Mäkinen (detail).

TOP RIGHT: Option Snowboards, 2007. Pro model for Joni Mäkinen.

BOTTOM LEFT: Burton Snowboards, 2007. Close-up of pro model for Jussi Oksanen.

BOTTOM RIGHT: Burton Snowboards, 2007. Pro model for Jussi Oksanen.

What other media do you work with besides graphic design?

I try to do one low-fi, zero-budget snowboard movie every year. It's just for fun and a nice documentation of the season. My movies feature only riders over thirty years old. Most of the riders and skaters in our movies are closer to forty now. We are getting old, but it doesn't stop the fun. You can check out the movies at www.vimeo.com/jarisalo.

Can you tell us more about what you're doing with the Spatial Experience project?

Spatial Experience is a project that I'm doing with my Swiss rider friends. It's all about leaving only your footprints in the snow. We encourage people to go riding with public transportation and hike up with snowshoes or by using a splitboard, and to enjoy the silence and pure nature without the crowds of the ski resorts. It's good to go up slowly; you start to observe and listen to nature in a different way than in ski resorts where there's always a rush to get the good pow turns before others.

The project will first focus on Swiss locations, and hopefully we can expand the project to other countries in the future. Environmental issues are close to my heart. I feel guilty about my own massive carbon footprint, so I'm trying to do something good and also change my own lifestyle in a more sustainable direction.

OPPOSITE PAGE, LEFT: Burton
Snowboards, 2005. Pro model for
Jussi Oksanen.

OPPOSITE PAGE, RIGHT: HEAD
Snowboards, 2009.

ABOVE: Watercolor T-shirt graphics.
Client: 686, 2010.

$\mathfrak{Styk}$ {INTERVIEW}

SEATTLE, WASHINGTON, U.S.A.

Born and raised in the small town of Grant, Nebraska, Styk graduated from the University of Nebraska in 1987 with a bachelor's degree in graphic design. He soon moved to Seattle, where at Burning Bush Studios his design clients included Comedy Central, Nintendo, and several major record companies including Rhino, Capitol, and Geffen. Styk then joined Ride Snowboards as creative director and held that position for many years. He is currently chief visual operations director and cofounder of Dept of Energy in Seattle, where he provides conceptual design direction for a variety of companies including Ride, Rossignol, and DC.

How many years did you work as art director for Ride Snowboards, and how did you get that job?
Eleven years, from 1995 to 2006. In 1995, I had a small design business with my partner, and we were asked by Ride to do board graphics for one of their pro models. We gave them some ideas and were asked to come to their headquarters.

When we got there, it was apparent they had no marketing office, and soon we were immersed into the brand, trying to help out where we could. After some time, they hired us internally.

Bernard Gervasoni, a board engineer for Ride, had a concept for a new board that lifted the rider higher out of the halfpipe, and you were asked to create graphics to help market it. What happened with that project?
This was driven by the engineering of the ollie power of the board. We came up with the name Protopipe, referring to another apparatus common to the snowboarding industry. The name came about due to the nature of the split in the middle of the tip and tail. This split in the board without reinforcement would eventually shatter without the pipe center grommet placed into the pocket of the split. Only six of these boards were made, and we designed the graphics, but the board was never marketed. The board reacted as we wanted but was another project that only makes the engineering historical archives.

OPPOSITE PAGE, LEFT: Styk in his
second love, a 1967 Chevy pickup,
Issaquah, Washington. Photo: Jynn
Hintz-Romano.

OPPOSITE PAGE, RIGHT: Serum
diecut base. Client: Ride Snowboards,
2001.

TOP: Kink denim sewing and woven
label. Client: Ride Snowboards, 2004.

RIGHT: Kink diecut base. Client: Ride
Snowboards, 2004.

*At Ride, you helped create the Kink Denim board,
one of the first boards using fabric material as a
top sheet. Describe the process of working with
new material when producing a prototype.*

At first, it was tough preventing the board's resin
from soaking through the denim top sheet. Peel
tests proved you could rip the resin-stained denim
from the top sheet. When the real denim top
approach was shelved in favor of a printed denim
graphic, one of my engineers figured out how to
laminate the denim's underside with a material that
prevented resin seepage and created a strong bond.
Having this built at the factory in China was the only
way to prove if it would work. The denim board that
was delivered from the factory passed top-sheet
peel and pull tests, and allowed it to go to market.
Through test rides, it was determined that snow
stuck to the denim unless it was treated, but then
the board became super heavy. We encouraged the
consumer to use Nikwax or another water-repellent
spray to prevent the snow from sticking. It was a
happy accident and many buyers began bleaching
the tops as they had with their jeans. This board

led us to perfect the process through complete lamination of the cloth used as a top sheet. This has become a mainstay in Ride's current graphic arsenal.

You produced a board graphic for the Timeless model, with science fiction illustrator Rodney Mathews, and also designed a board with Syd Mead, the conceptual designer for the sets of Blade Runner, TRON, and Alien, among other films. How did you develop those relationships, and were you happy with the results?

We'd always been a fan of Rodney's work. One day, I thought to just look him up. What I got was his art agent and they were willing to deal on the price and the licensing deal they thought they could get—but in snowboarding, the license agreement is thrown out the window because most companies can barely pay for graphics, let alone a license fee for each sale. Rodney was so amazing to work with that we used him on two models and he was willing to sign every deck he had done for us. It was an honor to work with Rodney.

When I contacted Syd Mead, he had no idea what a snowboard was. When we met in Seattle at one of his speaking engagements, I brought a snowboard with me and he was awestruck when he saw how big the snowboard was, "and it's such a vertical canvas!" We decided on some of his portfolio artwork, a rather wide painting that we could use across the entire model line. We then developed an interesting base from one of the characters in the painting. JJ Thomas happened to ride that model in the halfpipe that year and he lifted Syd's graphic on the podium when he received a bronze medal at the 2002 Winter Olympics in Salt Lake City. Syd doesn't follow snowboarding, but he was elated when he saw that image appearing across newspaper front pages for the next few days after the Olympics.

If you could collaborate with anyone in the world, who would that be?

Karim Rashid; I've always loved his work. His work and anyone else who is better than me and can teach me from what they've learned in life.

Looking back on your design career, is there one big break or project or person that you feel changed the course of your life?

One of my best friends and one of the most talented designers I've ever worked with I met while shopping for a designer to join us at Ride. I was speaking at Western Washington University and noticed this student more interested in sleep; it's how design students typically roll, due to lack of sleep. After talking to Mark "Fank" Fankhauser, I hired him at Ride. The best decision I ever made was to hire people more talented than I was. They always make you better. That collaboration went even further when Fank started suggesting other people that we should hire to create artwork.

Any advice you'd like to pass on to someone wanting to break into the industry?

Be persistent, stay in front of their faces, and always be humbled by what you learn along the journey. Oh, and always follow your heart . . . you can call it bullshit later!

OPPOSITE LEFT: Business top sheet. Client: Ride Snowboards, 2005.

OPPOSITE MIDDLE: Protopipe top sheet. Client: Ride Snowboards, 2000.

OPPOSITE RIGHT: Timeless top sheet (Rodney Matthews). Client: Ride Snowboards, 2000.

TOP LEFT: Kink diecut base (limited-edition colorway). Client: Ride Snowboards, 2006.

TOP RIGHT: Kink top sheet (limited-edition purple bass-boat glitter colorway). Client: Ride Snowboards, 2006.

Go with the Snow Aaron Draplin

PORTLAND, OREGON, U.S.A.

Aaron Draplin grew up in Detroit and developed an early interest in drawing, skateboarding, and snowboarding. At the end of his teens, he moved to Bend, Oregon, where he and his snowboard buddies would "make 'zines and grip-tape graphics and stickers." His first professional assignment was in fall 1993 for Solid Snowboards, designing the graphics for a pro-model board.

Draplin had an epiphany. He recalls, "The pro team came through Bend, and I saw the first prototype. We went up to Mt. Baker to ride, and I saw some kid whip by on one of my designs—I'll never forget the moment of seeing my little creation, out there in the world. That hooked me."

As the head of newly formed Draplindustries Design Co., Draplin explored many areas of graphic design, including lettering café signs and designing logos, and eventually attended the Minneapolis College of Art and Design where he received his design degree.

In 2000, he became art director of *Snowboarder* magazine and, during his tenure, created twenty-three issues of the magazine, winning the

2000 Primedia Art Director of the Year award. In 2004, following a two-year stint as senior designer at Cinco Design in Portland, Draplin founded Draplin Design Co. His client list includes Coal Headwear, the Union Binding Company, *Snowboard* magazine, Ride, Forum, Gnu, K2, and Burton Snowboards. Draplin is particularly strong in the area of logo design.

Draplin often browses his collection of books from the design masters, old encyclopedias, vintage manuals, modernist magazines, and "long-forgotten trash," as he says, for inspiration. "But the first idea you get is usually the best one, and the process of discovery often happens internally before you browse for ideas."

His advice for an aspiring snowboard designer is blunt: "Move to the mountains—now. You need to immerse yourself in the shred life—riding every day, learning the language, and living the lifestyle. Live it, and then work in it."

TOP LEFT: Gary and Aaron. Photo: Tim Zimmerman.

TOP RIGHT: Interior of DDC studio. Photo: Mike Basher.

ABOVE: *Snowboard* magazine cover, December 2008 issue.

LOGOS, LEFT TO RIGHT: South American Snow Sessions, 2006. South American Snow Sessions, 2006. Grenade Gloves, 2007. Gnu Altered Genetics, 2006. Cobra Dogs, 2007. Exit Real World, 2007.

LEFT: Gnu "Altered Genetics,"
2006–2007.

MIDDLE: Compatriot "Outra Vez,"
2009–2010.

RIGHT: Lib Tech "Travis Rice Pro
Model," 2007–2008.

Not My Problem
JMZ

GENEVA, SWITZERLAND

Swiss designer JMZ (Jim Zbinden) creates designs for snow, skate, and sport brands such as Nidecker, Zoo York skateboards, YES Snowboards, Burton Snow, UnInc, Nike, and Adidas. In addition to running Geneva-based skate shop Pulp68, which JMZ founded in 1995, he is art and marketing director for YES.NOW Snowboards.

JMZ enjoys playing with conceptual limits, citing as his favorite design project a board that was rejected by Burton UnInc. The board graphic, "Everybrand," incorporates a mash-up of competitors' logos. "I like to reinterpret old logos, people, and ads, probably because I come from skateboarding in the nineties, when you usually stole from other logos to do your own work."

It's no mystery to him why the board was rejected. "Nowadays, things are too serious— designs need to be approved by layers of committees and sales managers, so as to not offend anyone. Where's the fun? I design what I like. If you like it, cool. If you don't, that's cool, too. It's not my problem if you have no sense of humor!"

Although his work appears on many board brands, the Pulp68 shop allows JMZ the artistic freedom he cherishes. "I like retro games and design. My universe is mostly inspired by brands, movies, and classics from the eighties and nineties. You can explore my world through my boards for Pulp68."

JMZ has snowboarded since 1986, but avoids tricks and professional competitions after injuring his ankle in 1995 while skateboarding off season. "When I go snowboarding now," he says, "painkillers are my best buddy."

LEFT: Costco ID photo of Art Chantry

RIGHT: G Force snowboard design for K2 Snowboards, 1987

BOTTOM: The Rocket Mudhoney parody cover of Nevermind. Design: Chantry; photography: Karen Moskowitz, 1992.

Godfather of Grunge Design Art Chantry

SEATTLE, WASHINGTON, U.S.A.

If Neil Young is the godfather of grunge rock, Art Chantry is the godfather of grunge design. For more than thirty-five years, his thought-provoking and, at times, unconventional graphic creations have made him an iconic presence in the Pacific Northwest. A free-thinking artist working as a designer, Chantry is best known as the art director for the *Rocket*, a Seattle-based biweekly newspaper devoted to the local music scene. Beginning in 1984, and for the next ten years, Chantry helped design many memorable *Rocket* covers, including his famous Nirvana-*Nevermind* album parody, featuring grunge band Mudhoney. "That was one of the most technically difficult photo shoots I've ever worked on—we did it as a single shot, no gimmicks," Chantry recalls. During this period, he was also designing album covers and other graphics for Sub Pop and Estrus Records, contributing his strong visual ideas to the Pacific Northwest alternative music scene.

Although he recalls, "Nobody would hire me because my stuff was too fucking weird," he found his niche and has thrived. When much of the design field shifted toward the digital medium, Chantry survived by establishing himself as an "idea person" and by being anticomputer.

Though not as widely known as his music-based graphics, his sports industry designs are equally impressive. Not only did Chantry design one of the first commercially produced snowboards for ski manufacturer K2, he designed one of the first modern snowboards ever. In 1987, snowboarding was a new winter sport, and K2 asked Chantry to help create a board that would appeal to the youth market. His 100 percent analog design for K2's G Force snowboard was created using a photocopier

and a waxer, assembled as an old-fashioned mechanical. Today, Chantry's final designs are delivered to the client as digital files, but hand assembly is still his preferred creative method.

In the late 1990s, Chantry created the company identity and board logo for the SnoDad, a surfboard-style board designed to ride ungroomed snow. Though no longer in production, the SnoDad was a true backcountry board built for big waves of powder: a 5-foot (1.5 m) long, seven-ply maple deck with a rubber footpad, three fins arranged in a thruster pattern, and without bindings or metal edges. To ride, you simply laced up your favorite boots and jumped on. The surfboard-style leash attachment on the bottom of the board was designed to help keep the board with the rider during a wipeout. "It was the total punk rocker of snowboards," Chantry says.

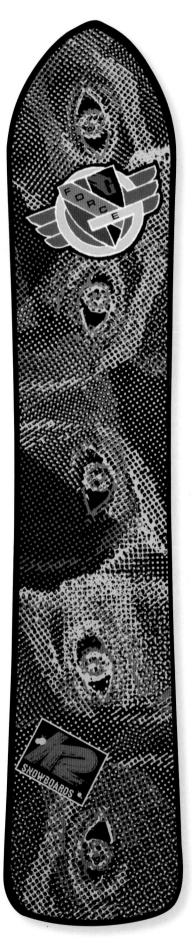

RIGHT: The Psycho wakeboard design for Jobe Sports. Designers: Chantry and Jamie Sheehan, 1994.

BELOW: Each Jobe Psycho wakeboard included free polarized eyeglasses—disguised as a hangtag—enabling customers to view the board in 3-D. Designers: Chantry and Jamie Sheehan, 1994.

BOTTOM: Sunglasses and packaging design for Oakley. Art director: Paul Schulte, 2009.

FAR RIGHT: The SnoDad, 1999.

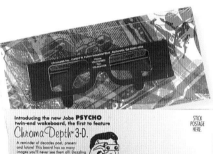

Fun with Animals & Robots
Ghica Popa

BUCHAREST, ROMANIA

Based in Bucharest, Romania, prolific graphic artist and creative director Ghica Popa crafts his own playful fantasy world of characters and images. Fascinated with the relationship of nature to technology and society, his visual output often includes industrial landscapes and interlocking networks of buildings populated by cartoonlike animals, both real and imagined, all oddly cheerful among the chaos. Airplanes flown by brave cats dive-bomb among fifties robots and smokestack-filled factory skylines.

After graduating from art school, Popa worked for eight years as an art director for what he calls the "fancy companies" (McCann Erickson; Leo Burnett) before becoming creative director of Bucharest's Punct Advertising. His clients include Procter & Gamble, Western Union, GE Money, Fanta, and Sprite, in addition to many Romanian clients. His work has won many design awards from advertising festivals around the world.

Popa describes his design influences as a blend of "science-fiction movies I watched as a kid, strange buildings, old futuristic cars, comic books, and art movements, from cubism to pop art."

Popa's playful images are seen on many media and in many contexts: album covers, comic strips, watchbands, coffee shop branding, posters, T-shirts, toys, cars, and, of course, snowboards. Popa's winning entry in a snowboard design competition by Artec was exhibited in the art gallery of Artec's booth at ISPO Winter 2009.

TOP: Ghica Popa in his studio, 2010. Photo: Alina Popa.

RIGHT: Board design, 2009. Winning design in a competition sponsored by Artec.
Board design submission, 2008. Finalist in the Burton Snowboard Design Contest.
Board design submission, 2007. Finalist in the Salomon Artwork Design Contest.

Mean Birds Amy Ruppel

ABOVE: Amy Ruppel in her Portland studio.

PORTLAND, OREGON, U.S.A.

Portland-based Amy Ruppel's dual love of art and science initially led her to consider a career in medical and science illustration, but she eventually found her true calling as an artist, illustrator, and surface designer. Ruppel has always been intrigued by colors and shapes derived from nature. Her work features an abundance of forests, flowers, and animals—especially birds. She initially drew the birds several years ago for a client who wanted to use avian silhouettes. The client only used a few examples, so

Ruppel was left with several birds that subsequently became the bread and butter of her artistic work. Although many of her designs and illustrations are admittedly "light and airy," she recently created a collection of dark and brooding birds, called Birds That Are Mean, which includes an image of a Canada goose that she calls "Asshole."

Ruppel also enjoys combining manual techniques with digital illustration. Her fine-art works combine the use of computer graphics with wax

and wood. She also plays with shapes and colors—all of the colored shapes in her work are digital slices of photos she has taken, an approach she also used for the snowboard she designed for Burton in 2008. She was recently approached by Gnu to design artwork for its 2009–2010 B-Real snowboard collection. Despite her success with snowboard graphic design, Ruppel is not a snowboarder herself: "I'm more of a spiked-cocoa-in-the-lodge kind of girl."

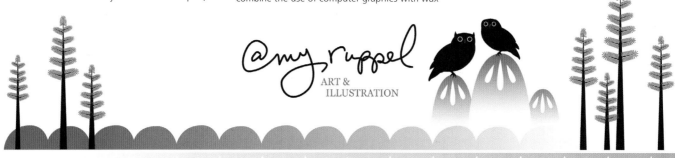

@amy ruppel
ART & ILLUSTRATION

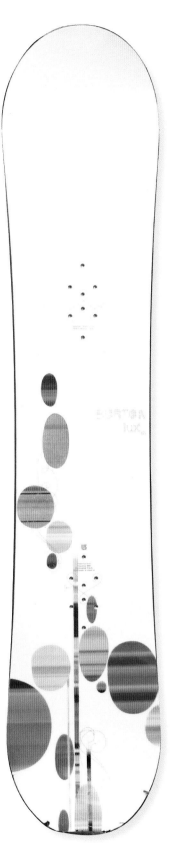

OPPOSITE PAGE, RIGHT TOP:
An example of Amy's encaustic illustration style, 2010.

OPPOSITE PAGE, RIGHT MIDDLE:
"Asshole," a selection from the Birds That Are Mean gallery show, 2009.

OPPOSITE PAGE, RIGHT BOTTOM:
Amy's wax station.

OPPOSITE PAGE, LOWER:
Signature and graphics pulled from Amy's website.

LEFT: Top and bottom board artwork for B-Real. Gnu Snowboards, 2009–2010.

RIGHT: Top and bottom board artwork for Burton Lux Women's snowboard series. Client: JDK, 2008.

TOP: Boards, left to right: Lowride,
Berzerker (2011), Slackcountry (2010),
and Agenda (2009). Client: Ride
Snowboards.

ABOVE: Pen-and-ink illustration:
"Colt 45."

OPPOSITE PAGE, LOWER:
Derek Muscat. Photo: Garry Hunt.

A Frame of White for the Canvas
Derek Muscat

ORANGEVILLE, ONTARIO, CANADA

For Canadian graphic designer Derek Muscat, snowboarding is both a passion and an artistic inspiration. Although he cites his general influences as family, friends, music, and film, "sliding down a snow-covered hill on a slab of wood, steel, and resin is the greatest contributor of all. It was, and always will be, a frame of white for the canvas below my feet."

With artistic skills honed at the Sheridan College for Illustration in Brampton, west of Toronto, Muscat submitted in 2003 a snowboard graphic for the first Snowboard Art Design Competition held in Steamboat Springs, Colorado, and cosponsored by Ride Snowboards. He won Best of Show and worked freelance with Ride for three years, starting with graphics for their 04/05 Lowride board. In 2006, Muscat jokingly approached creative director Mike Styskal and said, "Fuck, dude, just hire me full-time, already." Styk did.

Muscat's logos and graphics appear in and on many settings, including T-shirts and snowboards for Ride, 5150, Option, and Atomic; a logo for Planet Earth Clothing; and, perhaps in their bid for some street cred, a 2008 police cruiser for the Peel Regional Police in Ontario that includes some very retro racing stripes.

It is his continuing work with Ride that brings Muscat the most artistic satisfaction, allowing him to "have creative freedom within a strong direction provided by the creative director. I'm able to design full graphics from start to finish."

Muscat combines a fine drawing technique with color overlays and digital manipulation. "The way I work, all my graphics is very traditional. I start off with several thumbnails and submit them. Once the direction is set by the creative director, I then hand-illustrate everything with ink. I scan my work into Photoshop and then play, tweak, and build the graphic as though I'm creating a screen-printed poster. Then, I sometimes design the sidewall art to match the overall look for the board.

"The base graphic is next. In Illustrator, I design a multipiece diecut, like a big, colorful puzzle that is laser-fused together."

Bold Ideas, Bold Images

Michael Paddock

GOSHEN, NEW YORK, U.S.A.

Michael Paddock began his relationship to snow strictly as a rider, skiing the slopes of New York's Mount Peter before switching to snowboarding in winter 1989. As art director for Rome SDS (Snowboard Design Syndicate), Paddock admits, "What began as a substitute for skateboarding during winter months evolved into something that has driven a lot of the choices in my life."

Growing up in Warwick, New York, an hour outside Manhattan, Paddock took a graphic arts class while he was a senior in high school and then attended the College of Saint Rose in Albany, New York, from 1996 to 2000. He received a bachelor's degree in graphic design, and while in school was deeply involved in photography and screenprinting. After a short stint at an advertising agency near Boston, Paddock quit his job and moved west to Mammoth Lakes, California, where he met Josh Reid, cofounder of Waterbury, Vermont–based snowboard company Rome SDS. Paddock began as Rome's staff photographer, which soon led to designing a board graphic with Sean Carmody.

Since 2004, Paddock has worked full-time as Rome's art director and photographer. He spends ten months of the year working on future collections for boards, boots, and bindings, typically creating more than half of the hard goods work for a collection, and he is responsible for all the product photography used by the brand.

Paddock's approach to graphic assemblage appears all inclusive. "Any or all of the following is generally incorporated: ink, markers, glue sticks, spray paint, X-Acto blades, Band-Aids, charcoal,

found objects, screen prints, original photos, pencils, found photos, blood, sweat, and tears."

So, what is his design sequence? "Everything starts with a pencil and paper. I will typically refine the idea with more sketching before getting it into the computer, and then a lot of back and forth between analog and digital. Elements will be printed out, cut up, drawn on, and collaged together to get the right look and feel before being scanned back into digital. Then I do a bit of Photoshop work before heading into Illustrator, where most of the finalizing is done."

OPPOSITE PAGE, LEFT: Paddock in his home office, Goshen, New York, October 2010. Photo: Storm Sasaki.

OPPOSITE PAGE, RIGHT: Artifact original art. Client: Rome SDS. Photo: Paddock, 2005.

ABOVE, LEFT TO RIGHT:
Base graphic for Artifact Live Nude Girls board. Client: Rome SDS, 2008.
Base graphic for Artifact Street Justice board. Client: Rome SDS, 2009.
Base graphic for Artifact Jerk Moves board. Client: Rome SDS, 2010.
Base graphic for Artifact Dealin' board. Client: Rome SDS, 2007.
Top-sheet graphic for Artifact Dealin' board. Client: Rome SDS, 2007.

Rome Snowboard Design Syndicate
The 2011 Postermania
U.S.A.

Soldier Design
Mix Tapes
U.S.A.

Soldier Design
On Point
U.S.A.

K2 Snowboarding
Va Va Voom, Top & Base
U.S.A.

K2 Snowboarding
Fastplant
U.S.A.

K2 Snowboarding
Slayblade
U.S.A.

Soldier Design
Hippi Dandy Shatter
U.S.A.

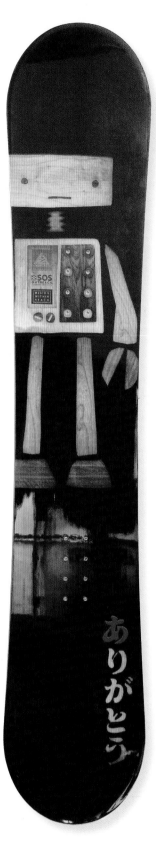
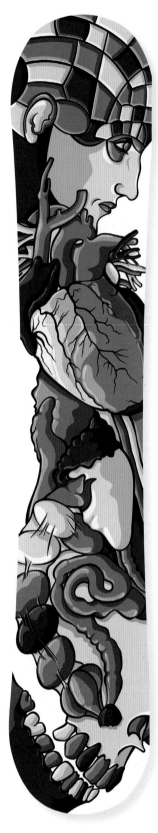

Emil Kozak
Salomon
Spain

Melissa Laine Scotton
Cherryblossom
U.S.A.

Turnstyle
Untitled
U.S.A.

Soyuze
Untitled
Italy

Jager Di Paola Kemp Design
Custom 56, Top & Base
U.S.A.

Jager Di Paola Kemp Design
Conflict, Top & Base
U.S.A.

Jager Di Paola Kemp Design
Unlnc 56 & Love55
U.S.A.

Jager Di Paola Kemp Design
Custom 64, Top & Base
U.S.A.

Jager Di Paola Kemp Design
EZL 58
U.S.A.

Jager Di Paola Kemp Design
Spinster 146
U.S.A.

Super Top Secret
Jdub 2008
U.S.A.

Super Top Secret
Imperial
U.S.A.

Super Top Secret
Fuse Sticker
U.S.A.

Super Top Secret
District
U.S.A.

Super Top Secret
Jdub 2009
U.S.A.

Super Top Secret
Vandal, Top & Base
U.S.A.

Aloha Studios
Various, Top & Base
Greece

Aloha Studios
Lights, Top & Base
Greece

SoupGraphix
Manic 2, Top & Base
U.S.A.

Aloha Studios
Luvs Nature, Top & Base
Greece

Aloha Studios
Luvs Nature, Top & Base
Greece

SoupGraphix
Manic 1, Top & Base
U.S.A.

SoupGraphix
Flow 2
U.S.A.

Hannah Stouffer
Barrett
U.S.A.

Hannah Stouffer
Tiger
U.S.A.

Hannah Stouffer
Barrett
U.S.A.

Hannah Stouffer
Sims Artist Series
U.S.A.

Ashton Howard	**Randi Meredith**	**onetreeink**	**onetreeink**		**Tomato Košir**	**Roman Ražman**	**Melissa Laine Scotton**
Untitled	*Booty Pirate*	*Samurai Board*	*Innerself*		*Irony, Top & Base*	*Stainless*	*Tree*
U.S.A.	U.S.A.	U.S.A.	U.S.A.		Slovenia	Slovenia	U.S.A.

The Medium Control	**The Medium Control**	**LaMar Snowboards**	**LaMar Snowboards**	**LaMar Snowboards**
Merits, Top & Base	*Collective, Top & Base*	*Fisher*	*Protocol*	*Quest, Top & Base*
U.S.A.	U.S.A.	U.S.A.	U.S.A.	U.S.A.

Valhalla
Pivot, Top & Base
U.S.A.

Valhalla
Exeter 165
U.S.A.

Valhalla
Revival 135
U.S.A.

Valhalla
Polarity
U.S.A.

Valhalla
Mighty D
U.S.A.

Valhalla
Axum 153
U.S.A.

The beautiful design
Format 2009, Top & Base
U.S.A.

The beautiful design
Brigade 2009, Top & Base
U.S.A.

The beautiful design
Skyla 2010, Top
U.S.A.

The beautiful design
Skyla 2010, Base
U.S.A.

The beautiful design
Podium 2010, Top & Base
U.S.A.

The beautiful design
Siren 2009, Top & Base
U.S.A.

I-Manifest
MOD, Top & Base
U.S.A.

M80 Design LLC
Vita
U.S.A.

Turnstyle
Untitled
U.S.A.

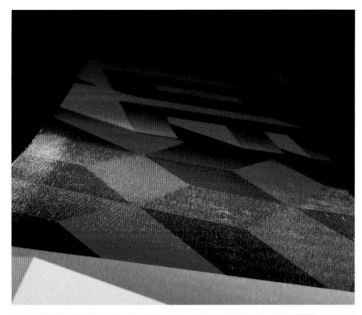

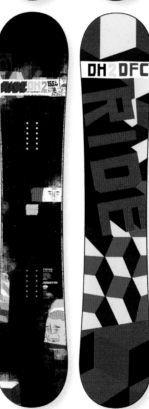

Ride Snowboards
DH 2009, Top & Base
U.S.A.

Ride Snowboards
DH, Base
U.S.A.

Ride Snowboards
DH2
U.S.A.

Ride Snowboards
DH
U.S.A.

Ride Snowboards
DH 2008, Top & Base
U.S.A.

Ride Snowboards
DH2
U.S.A.

Paul Brown
Shadow, Top & Base
U.S.A.

Paul Brown
Austin Smith 56, Top & Base
U.S.A.

Paul Brown
Eero Pro 55, Top
U.S.A.

Paul Brown
Eero Pro 55, Base
U.S.A.

Paul Brown
Rook 54
U.S.A.

Paul Brown
Rook 56
U.S.A.

Paul Brown
Rook 58
U.S.A.

Paul Brown
Rook 52
U.S.A.

Paul Brown
ProOne Kooley 52, Top & Base
U.S.A.

Paul Brown
Haze 54W, Top & Base
U.S.A.

Paul Brown
Pro Series 56 Eero
U.S.A.

Paul Brown
Pro Series 56 Smith
U.S.A.

Paul Brown
Pro Series 53 Kooley
U.S.A.

Paul Brown
Pro Series 59 Fox
U.S.A.

Paul Brown
Pro Series 49 Maas
U.S.A.

Paul Brown
Pro Series 53 Keller
U.S.A.

Michael Paddock
LoFi Rocker
U.S.A.

Morning Breath
Untitled
U.S.A.

Morning Breath
Untitled
U.S.A.

Morning Breath
Untitled
U.S.A.

Morning Breath
Untitled
U.S.A.

Morning Breath
Untitled
U.S.A.

SoupGraphix
Flow 6
U.S.A.

SoupGraphix
Flow 5
U.S.A.

SoupGraphix
Flow 7
U.S.A.

SoupGraphix
Flow 1
U.S.A.

ACKNOWLEDGMENTS

First, we are grateful for new technology—the Internet made it possible for us to connect with people from almost every continent on the planet. Without the Internet and social networking sites such as Facebook, we would have never found Gustavo Giler, Taro Tamai, Macarrão, Mzwandile Buthelezi, Ghica Popa, Murray Walding, Matt Barr, and many others.

Secondly, a big thank you to all the contributors for answering our emails and phone calls and providing the information and images that became this book. A hearty thanks to the people who helped us connect to other people: Ed Fotheringham (Paul McNeil), Eva Collado (Murray Walding), Marc Hostetter (Matt Barr), Kye Fitzgerald (Martin Worthington), Greg Escalante (Rich Harbour), George Estrada (Damion Hayes), Chris Magpoc (Arne Knudson), Arne Knudson (Jeannie Chesser), Jair Bortoleto (Macarrão), and Mike Styskal (Max Jenke, Derek Muscat, and Grain Surfboards).

Special thanks to Josilaine Alves for translating Portuguese into English, and to Shogo Ota for translating the Japanese interviews. A heartfelt thanks goes to Marc Hostetter (Skate), Murray Walding (Surf) and Matt Barr (Snow) for writing the introductions for each book section.

Inside the World of Board Graphics would not have happened without the contributions of the following writers: Damion Hayes, Charlotte West, Shogo Ota, and Marty Jourard. In addition to his writing contribution, Marty's careful editing made us sound like better writers. Damion, Charlotte, Shogo, and Marty put in a tremendous amount of time and energy for which we express our gratitude. Without their collective efforts this project would have never gotten off the ground.

Finally we wish to thank our Rockport support staff, and especially our editor Emily Potts, who originally approached us to do a different book. When we turned that down she asked what we wanted to do instead, and we promised something different. The result is this book.

CONTRIBUTORS

AUTHOR BIOS

ROBYNNE RAYE

Robynne Raye is cofounder of Seattle-based Modern Dog Design Co. For more than two decades, Raye has lectured and taught workshops, in both the United States and abroad. Her design work has been exhibited internationally and is in the archives of major libraries and in museum collections worldwide. She is author of *My Favorite Shoes* and coauthor of *Modern Dog: 20 Years of Poster Art*. She currently teaches typography and packaging design courses at Cornish College of the Arts in Seattle.

MICHAEL STRASSBURGER

Michael Strassburger is cofounder of Seattle-based Modern Dog Design Co. While a sense of humor is almost always present in Strassburger's work, he is nonetheless very serious in his approach to design. His work has been profiled in numerous publications, museums, and libraries, both nationally and internationally. Strassburger is coauthor of *Oh Crap, I'm Having a Baby* and *Modern Dog: 20 Years of Poster Art*. Currently, he is an adjunct instructor at Cornish College of the Arts in Seattle.

MARTY JOURARD

Marty Jourard received his bachelor's degree in English from the University of Washington in 1997. In addition to writing extensively on music through his columns and feature articles in the *Rocket*, *Gig*, *Tape Op*, and other music periodicals, he is the author of *Start Your Own Band* and *The Marty Method*, a piano and music instruction book. He likes words, loves sentences, and is in awe of paragraphs.

DAMION HAYES

Damion Hayes is an accomplished curator, a gallerist, and a lifelong skateboarder. As the director of renowned art gallery BLVD, he is able to explore the edges of pop culture where street art and board culture intersect, forming the aesthetic movement dubbed urban contemporary. Hayes has curated projects for Red Bull, Bumbershoot Arts Festival, Indiecade, Desmadre Arte, and *Dodge and Burn* magazine. He is currently searching for the perfect place to skate on a rainy day

SHOGO OTA

Shogo Ota grew up snowboarding in the mountains of Gifu, Japan. He came to the United States in 2001 and graduated with a bachelor's degree in fine art from the University of Idaho. Since 2006, he has worked as a designer and illustrator at Seattle-based Modern Dog, where he stretches his creative muscles on a variety of projects.

CHARLOTTE WEST

Charlotte West is a Seattle-based writer who recently returned to the United States after six years in Stockholm, Sweden. She covers design and architecture for publications such as *Computer Arts*, *Print*, *Icon*, and *Men's Journal*. She is working on a book about young Eastern European graphic designers.

Unknown lettering artist from Ulu Watu Beach, Indonesia.
Photo: Josh Oakley.